Hot Sauce Prep for Chili Lovers

The 365-Day Spicy Cookbook with Simple Recipes to Make Every Dish Irresistible

Kent Harlen

Table of contents

INTRODUCTION

Welcome to the fiery world of hot sauces, where each drop carries a burst of flavor and a kick of heat that can transform any dish. If you're reading this, you're likely someone who enjoys the thrill of a spicy bite and is ready to dive deeper into the art of making hot sauces. This book is your guide to exploring a diverse array of recipes, designed to tantalize your taste buds and broaden your culinary horizons.

Imagine the satisfaction of crafting your own hot sauces, tailored precisely to your taste. From the mild and tangy to the scorchingly hot, you'll find recipes that cater to every heat tolerance and flavor preference. Each sauce tells its own story, drawing inspiration from various cultures and culinary traditions around the globe.

Hot sauce enthusiasts know that the right sauce can make a meal unforgettable. Whether you're drizzling smoky chipotle sauce over grilled meats or adding a splash of tangy jalapeño sauce to your tacos, the perfect hot sauce can bring out the best in your food. This book is filled with easy-to-follow recipes, with ingredients that are accessible and affordable, ensuring you can create amazing sauces in your own kitchen.

Crafting hot sauce is both an art and a science. You'll learn about different types of chili peppers, their heat levels, and how they contribute to the overall flavor of a sauce. This knowledge will empower you to experiment with different combinations, adjusting heat and flavor to suit your preference. Each recipe in this book is a starting point, encouraging you to tweak and refine until you've created your perfect sauce.

Sharing your homemade sauces with friends and family can be incredibly rewarding. Imagine the delight on their faces when they taste your creations. Whether you're a novice in the kitchen or an experienced cook, you'll find recipes that inspire you and help you develop your skills.

So grab your apron, gather your ingredients, and get ready to spice up your life with homemade hot sauces!

1. EQUIPMENT FOR MAKING HOT SAUCES

The right equipment can make the process smoother and more enjoyable. Let's dive into the tools you'll need to get started.

- A **high-quality blender** is a must-have for smooth, well-emulsified hot sauces. Invest in one with variable speed settings.

- Furthermore a **heavy-bottomed pot**, such as stainless steel, ensures even heat distribution, perfect for simmering and reducing sauces.

- To prepare your ingredients, a **sharp chef's knife** and a sturdy **cutting board** are indispensable. A well-balanced knife makes chopping large quantities of vegetables easier and safer. For those particularly hot peppers, consider using a **dedicated cutting board and knife** to avoid cross-contaminating other foods with capsaicin.

- Another important item is a pair of gloves, since capsaicin can cause severe irritation to your skin and eyes. **Disposable nitrile gloves** are a good choice as they provide a barrier without compromising dexterity.

- For achieving a smooth consistency, a **fine-mesh sieve or strainer** is essential. This tool helps remove seeds and larger chunks.

- Fermentation enthusiasts will need a few additional tools. A set of **fermentation weights and airlock lids** can help you create the perfect environment for beneficial bacteria to thrive. **Glass jars** are preferred for fermenting.

- A **digital pH meter** is another excellent investment. This tool allows you to measure the acidity of your sauce, which is important for both flavor and preservation.

- Bottling your hot sauce is the final step in the process, and having the right equipment makes it easier. A **funnel set,** particularly one with a wide mouth, helps you transfer your sauce into bottles without spilling. Glass bottles with airtight caps are ideal for storing your finished product.

- **Waterproof labels and a fine-tip permanent marker** are useful for noting the date, ingredients, and heat level of each batch.

- Cleaning up after making hot sauce is straightforward if you have the right tools. A **bottle brush** is essential for thoroughly cleaning bottles and jars, especially if you plan to reuse them. This ensures that no residue is left behind that could affect the taste of your next batch.

- A **thermometer** is useful for precise cooking. Some hot sauces require cooking to a specific temperature to achieve the desired consistency and flavor.

- An **immersion blender** can be a handy alternative to a traditional blender, especially for small batches.

2. TIPS AND TRICKS FOR MAKING HOT SAUCES

Master the art of hot sauce making with these expert tips and tricks, ensuring every batch is flavorful, balanced, and fiery.

Fresh peppers, garlic, and onions enhance the taste and ensure your sauce is vibrant and robust. Opt for organic produce when possible to avoid pesticides and maximize flavor.

It's essential to understand the heat levels of different peppers. The Scoville scale, which measures the capsaicin concentration, helps you gauge the spiciness.

PEPPER	BOTANICAL NAME	HEAT LEVEL (SHU)	DESCRIPTION
Bell Pepper	Capsicum annuum	0	Sweet, mild, and used in salads, and stuffed dishes
Banana Pepper	Capsicum annuum	0-500	Mild, tangy, often pickled and used as a condiment.
Pimento (Cherry Pepper)	Capsicum annuum	100-500	Sweet, mild, used in cheese spreads, and stuffed olives.
Pepperoncini	Capsicum annuum	100-500	Mild, tangy, often pickled and used in salads and sandwiches.
Anaheim Pepper	Capsicum annuum	500-2,500	Mild, slightly sweet, used in Southwestern and Mexican dishes.

Poblano Pepper	Capsicum annuum	1,000-2,000	Mild, rich flavor, commonly used roasted or stuffed in dishes like chiles rellenos.
Pasilla Pepper	Capsicum annuum	1,000-2,500	Mild to medium, with a smoky, rich flavor, often used in mole sauces.
Jalapeño Pepper	Capsicum annuum	2,500-8,000	Popular in Mexican cuisine, used fresh, pickled, or smoked (as chipotle).
Serrano Pepper	Capsicum annuum	10,000-23,000	Hotter than jalapeños, used in salsas and sauces.
Cayenne Pepper	Capsicum annuum	30,000-50,000	Often dried and ground into powder, used in spicy dishes and as a seasoning.
Tabasco Pepper	Capsicum frutescens	30,000-50,000	Used to make Tabasco sauce, with a sharp, spicy flavor.
Thai Chili (Bird's Eye Chili)	Capsicum annuum	50,000-100,000	Small, very hot, used in Thai and Southeast Asian cuisine.
Chiltepin Pepper	Capsicum annuum var. glabriusculum	50,000-100,000	Tiny, very hot, often considered the mother of all modern chili peppers.

Habanero Pepper	Capsicum chinense	100,000-350,000	Extremely hot with a fruity flavor, used in hot sauces and Caribbean dishes.
Scotch Bonnet Pepper	Capsicum chinense	100,000-350,000	Similar to habanero in heat and flavor, commonly used in Caribbean cuisine.
Ghost Pepper (Bhut Jolokia)	Capsicum chinense	855,000-1,041,427	One of the hottest peppers in the world, used sparingly in very spicy dishes.
7 Pot Douglah Pepper	Capsicum chinense	1,000,000-1,800,000	Extremely hot, with a rich, nutty flavor, used in very spicy hot sauces.
Carolina Reaper Pepper	Capsicum chinense	1,400,000-2,200,000	Currently holds the Guinness World Record for the hottest chili pepper, used in extreme hot sauces.

To significantly **deepen the flavor** of your hot sauce you can **roast your ingredients**. Roasting peppers, garlic, and tomatoes before blending adds a smoky, caramelized taste that elevates the final product. Simply place the ingredients on a baking sheet and roast them in the oven until they are slightly charred.

Incorporate acids like **vinegar** or **citrus juice** to enhance tanginess and serve as a preservative. **Vinegar**, in particular, helps **extend the shelf life** of your sauce. **Lime or lemon** juice can **brighten the flavor** profile.

Balancing heat with sweetness can create a more palatable sauce. Ingredients like **honey**, **brown sugar**, or **fruits** can counteract the heat and add depth.

Fermentation is another excellent method for adding complexity to your hot sauce. Allowing the sauce to ferment for a few days at room temperature can develop deeper, more nuanced flavors.

Using a **high-speed blender** ensures your sauce is **smooth and well-emulsified**. A consistent texture is important for a professional-quality hot sauce. If you prefer a chunkier sauce, pulse the blender instead of using it continuously.

Furthermore, when creating hot sauces, **it's wise to work in small** batches to find the flavors that suit your palate. This approach allows you to experiment with different ingredients and spice levels without committing to a large quantity.

Experiment with spices to add unique twists to your hot sauce. Common additions include cumin, coriander, and smoked paprika. These spices can complement the heat and add layers of flavor. Toasting whole spices before grinding them releases essential oils, enhancing their aroma.

Make sure to taste and **adjust** your **sauce during** the **cooking process**. Flavor development happens at every stage, so taste your sauce periodically and make adjustments as needed. Adding salt, sugar, or additional peppers can tweak the flavor to your liking.

Labeling Tips

Clear and informative labels are a great help in keeping track of your hot sauces. This helps you remember the details of each batch and provides useful information to anyone using the sauce.

1. **Include Key Details**:
   - **Name**
   - **Date**
   - **Ingredients**: highlight any unusual or allergenic items.
   - **Heat Level**: use terms like "mild," "medium," "hot," and "extra hot."
   - **pH Level**
2. **Design and Durability**:
   - **Waterproof Labels** to prevent smudging and fading.
   - **Clear Printing**

Accommodating Guests with Low Spice Tolerance

When hosting guests, it's considerate to provide options that cater to different spice tolerances. Here are some tips to ensure everyone enjoys their meal:

1. **Offer a Variety of Sauces**:
   - **Mild Options**: Prepare milder hot sauces that still pack flavor without overwhelming heat. Consider sauces based on milder peppers like poblanos.
   - **Heat Adjustments**: Have sauces of varying heat levels available, from mild to extra hot, so guests can choose according to their preference.
2. **Provide Clear Information**:
   - **Labels**: Clearly label hot sauces with their spice levels.
   - **Taste Tests**: Offer small samples of each sauce for guests to try before they commit to adding them to their food.
3. **Balance with Mild Dishes**:
   - **Pairings**: Serve milder dishes alongside spicy ones.
   - **Neutral Bases**: Provide a variety of sides like rice, bread, or vegetables that can help moderate the spice level when eaten together with hot sauce.
4. **Customization Options**:
   - **DIY Sauces**: Set up a station where guests can mix their own hot sauces, combining milder and hotter varieties to suit their taste.
   - **On the Side**: Serve hot sauce on the side rather than mixing it into dishes.

3. COMMON MISTAKES WHILE MAKING HOT SAUCE

Making hot sauce at home is an enjoyable and rewarding process, but beginners often encounter a few pitfalls. Understanding these common mistakes can help you avoid them and create a perfect hot sauce every time.

One frequent error is **not balancing** the **heat with other flavors**. Relying solely on the heat of the peppers can result in a one-dimensional sauce. Incorporating sweet, sour, and salty elements can create a more complex and enjoyable flavor profile.

Another mistake is **overcooking the ingredients**. Peppers, especially, can lose their vibrant taste and color if cooked for too long. Simmer the ingredients just until they are soft enough to blend, preserving their fresh flavors.

You shouldn't ignore the **role of pH** in preservation, as it can lead to a hot sauce that spoils quickly. A digital pH meter is a valuable tool for any hot sauce maker. It allows you to measure the acidity of your sauce accurately. To use it, simply take a small sample of your hot sauce and dip the probe of the pH meter into the sample. If the pH is above 4.6, you can adjust it by adding more acidic ingredients until you reach the desired level. Maintaining the correct pH is not only about safety but also about the quality and taste of your hot sauce. During fermentation, the natural bacteria will produce lactic acid, which helps to lower the pH. It's a good practice to check the pH before bottling to ensure it is within the safe range. If you're fermenting your hot sauce, keep it in a clean environment to prevent contamination by undesirable bacteria or mold.

In addition to using a pH meter, maintaining **good hygiene practices** during preparation, fermentation, and bottling stages is crucial. Sterilizing your equipment, using clean utensils, and storing your sauce in sterilized bottles with airtight seals will help maintain its quality and extend its shelf life.

Capsaicin, the compound responsible for the heat in peppers, can burn your skin and cause discomfort. Always **wear gloves** and **avoid touching** your face, especially your eyes, while preparing the peppers. Washing your hands thoroughly afterward is also a good practice.

Don't overlook the importance of **tasting and adjusting** throughout the process as it can lead to an unbalanced sauce. Taste your sauce at various stages and make adjustments as needed. Remember that the flavors may intensify as the sauce sits, so it's better to start with a lighter hand and adjust gradually.

Another common mistake is using **poor-quality ingredients**. Fresh, high-quality peppers, garlic, and other ingredients make a significant difference in the taste of your sauce.

My last advice is that **failing to experiment and have fun** with the process can limit your creativity. Hot sauce making is an art, and there's plenty of room to explore different flavors and techniques. Don't be afraid to try new pepper combinations, add unique spices, or incorporate unexpected ingredients. Each batch is an opportunity to learn and improve.

ATTENTION!

In most hot sauce recipes, the fermentation process is optional but highly recommended for those seeking to enhance the depth and complexity of flavors, as said earlier. To ensure safety during fermentation, as mentioned earlier, it's crucial to maintain the **pH level below 4.6**, as this acidic environment inhibits the growth of harmful bacteria. If the pH rises above 4.6, consider adding more vinegar or citrus juice to lower it.

1: CLASSIC FRESH RED HOT SAUCE

Yield: Approximately 1.5 cups	Prep time: 5 minutes	Scoville: 2,500 - 8,000 SHU

Ingredients

- 8 red Fresno peppers, stemmed and seeded
- 2 large red bell peppers, stemmed and seeded
- 3 cloves garlic, minced
- 1/4 cup white vinegar
- 1/4 cup fresh lemon juice
- 2 tablespoons olive oil
- 1 teaspoon salt
- 1/2 teaspoon smoked paprika (optional for added depth)

Instructions

1. *Preparation of Ingredients:*
   - Stem and seed the red Fresno peppers and red bell peppers. To save time, you can chop them roughly since they will be blended. Mince the garlic cloves.
2. *Blending:*
   - In a high-speed blender or food processor, combine the chopped Fresno peppers, red bell peppers, minced garlic, white vinegar, lemon juice, olive oil, salt, and smoked paprika (if using).
   - Blend on high until the mixture is smooth and well combined. This should take just about a minute.
3. *Adjusting Consistency:*
   - If the sauce is too thick, add a small amount of vinegar or lemon juice to reach your desired consistency. The sauce should be smooth and easily pourable.
4. *Tasting and Adjusting:*
   - Taste the sauce and adjust the seasoning as needed.

Store in the refrigerator, where it will keep fresh for up to two weeks.

Nutritional Information (per tablespoon): Calories: 10, Total Fat: 1g, Sodium: 90mg, Total Carbohydrates: 1g, Sugars: 0.5g, Protein: 0g

Tips

- This hot sauce is ideal for adding a burst of fresh, spicy flavor to your favorite dishes in just 5 minutes. Drizzle it over tacos, pizza, eggs, or grilled vegetables for an instant flavor boost.
- For extra heat, you can leave the seeds in the Fresno peppers or add a pinch of cayenne pepper to the blend.

2: JALAPEÑO-CUCUMBER HOT SAUCE

Yield: Approximately 2 cups	Prep Time: 5 minutes	Scoville: 2,500 - 8,000 SH

Ingredients

- 8 jalapeño peppers, stemmed and chopped
- 1 medium cucumber, peeled and chopped
- 3 cloves garlic, minced
- 1/2 cup apple cider vinegar
- 1/4 cup lime juice
- 1 tablespoon honey
- 1 teaspoon salt
- 1/2 cup water

Instructions

1. *Preparation of Ingredients:*
   - Stem and chop the jalapeño peppers. Peel and chop the cucumber, and mince the garlic cloves.
2. *Blending:*
   - In a high-speed blender or food processor, combine the chopped jalapeño peppers, cucumber, minced garlic, apple cider vinegar, lime juice, honey, salt, and water.
   - Blend on high until the mixture is smooth. The cucumber adds a refreshing element, while the jalapeños bring heat and flavor.
3. *Adjusting Consistency:*
   - If the sauce is too thick, add more water a tablespoon at a time until the desired consistency is reached. The sauce should be smooth and slightly thick, with a vibrant green color.
4. *Tasting and Adjusting:*
   - Taste the sauce and adjust the seasoning as necessary. Add more salt, honey, or lime juice to balance the flavors according to your preference.

Store in the refrigerator, where it will stay fresh for up to two weeks.

Nutritional Information (per tablespoon): Calories: 8, Total Fat: 0g, Sodium: 90mg, Total Carbohydrates: 2g, Sugars: 1g, Protein: 0g

Tips

- This quick, fresh hot sauce is perfect for adding a refreshing, spicy kick to grilled meats, fish tacos, or even as a zesty salad dressing.

3: TOMATO HOT SAUCE

Yield: Approximately 1.5 cups	Prep Time: 5 minutes	Scoville: 2,500 - 10,000 SHU

Ingredients

- 4 ripe tomatoes, chopped
- 2 tablespoons tomato paste
- 2 red chili peppers (such as Fresno or serrano), stemmed and seeded
- 2 cloves garlic, minced
- 2 tablespoons white vinegar
- 1 tablespoon olive oil
- 1 teaspoon salt
- 1/2 teaspoon sugar (optional, to balance acidity)

Instructions

1. *Preparation of Ingredients:*
   - Chop the ripe tomatoes and stem and seed the chili peppers. Mince the garlic cloves.
2. *Blending:*
   - In a high-speed blender or food processor, combine the chopped tomatoes, tomato paste, chili peppers, minced garlic, white vinegar, olive oil, salt, and sugar (if using).
   - Blend the mixture on high until smooth. The tomato paste adds depth and richness, while the fresh tomatoes provide a vibrant, juicy base.
3. *Adjusting Consistency:*
   - If the sauce is too thick, add a little more vinegar or a splash of water until you reach your desired consistency. The sauce should be smooth and slightly thick, with a bright red color.
4. *Tasting and Adjusting:*
   - Taste the sauce and adjust the seasoning if necessary.

Store in the refrigerator, where it will keep fresh for up to one week.

Nutritional Information (per tablespoon): Calories: 8, Total Fat: 0.5g, Sodium: 90mg, Total Carbohydrates: 1g, Sugars: 0.5g, Protein: 0g

Tips

- Use this sauce as a base for pasta, a topping for grilled vegetables, or a dip for crusty bread.
- If you want a spicier kick, add more chili peppers or keep the seeds in.

4: AVOCADO-JALAPEÑO HOT SAUCE

Yield: Approximately 2 cups	Prep Time: 15 minutes	Scoville: 2,500 - 8,000 SHU

Ingredients

- 2 ripe avocados, peeled and pitted
- 4 jalapeño peppers
- 2 cloves garlic, minced
- 1/2 cup fresh cilantro, chopped
- 1/2 cup lime juice
- 1/4 cup white vinegar
- 1 teaspoon salt
- 1 tablespoon honey
- 1/4 cup water

Instructions

1. *Preparation:*
   - Remove the stems and chop the peppers. Peel and pit the avocados, and mince the garlic. Chop the cilantro.
2. *Blending:*
   - Combine the avocados, chopped jalapeño peppers, garlic, cilantro, lime juice, white vinegar, salt, honey, and water in a blender.
   - Blend until smooth. If the sauce is too thick, add more water a tablespoon at a time until the desired consistency is reached.
3. *Adjusting Flavor:*
   - Taste the sauce and adjust the seasoning as needed. Add more salt or lime juice to balance the flavor to your liking.

The sauce can be kept refrigerated for up to a week due to the fresh avocado.

Nutritional Information (per tablespoon): Calories: 15, Total Fat: 1g, Sodium: 75mg, Total Carbohydrates: 2g, Sugars: 0.5g, Protein: 0.2g

Tips

- For a milder sauce, reduce the number of jalapeño peppers or substitute with milder varieties like Anaheim peppers.
- This creamy and tangy sauce pairs well with tacos, grilled fish, and as a dip for chips and vegetables.
- For an extra burst of flavor, try adding a teaspoon of cumin or smoked paprika to the blender.

5: FRESH CILANTRO-LIME HOT SAUCE

Yield: Approximately 1.5 cups	Prep Time: 15 minutes	Scoville: 10,000 - 23,000 SHU

Ingredients

- 8 serrano peppers, stemmed and seeded
- 1 cup fresh cilantro leaves, packed
- 1/4 cup fresh lime juice
- 2 tablespoons white wine vinegar
- 3 cloves garlic, minced
- 1/4 cup olive oil
- 1 teaspoon salt
- 1/2 teaspoon ground cumin
- Zest of 1 lime

Instructions

1. *Preparation of Ingredients:*
   - Stem and seed the serrano peppers. For those who enjoy a bit more heat, consider leaving some seeds in.
   - Rinse and dry the cilantro leaves, and peel the garlic cloves.
2. *Blending:*
   - In a high-speed blender or food processor, combine the serrano peppers, cilantro leaves, garlic, lime juice, white wine vinegar, olive oil, salt, ground cumin, and lime zest.
   - Blend the mixture on high until smooth. The olive oil will help emulsify the sauce, giving it a smooth, creamy texture.
   - If the sauce is too thick, add a little more lime juice or vinegar to reach your desired consistency.
3. *Tasting and Adjusting:*
   - Taste the sauce and adjust seasoning if needed. Add more salt or lime juice to balance the flavors according to your preference.

Store in the refrigerator, where it will keep fresh for up to two weeks.

Nutritional Information (per tablespoon): Calories: 15, Total Fat: 1g, Sodium: 95mg, Total Carbohydrates: 1g, Sugars: 0g, Protein: 0g

Tips

- This fresh cilantro-lime hot sauce is vibrant and zesty, perfect for drizzling over tacos, grilled meats, or seafood. The combination of serrano peppers and cilantro provides a bright heat that complements a variety of dishes.
- For a twist, consider adding a splash of tequila or mezcal to the blend for an extra layer of flavor that pairs well with the lime and cilantro.

6: JALAPEÑO-LIME HOT SAUCE

Yield: 2 cups	Prep Time: 15 minutes	Scoville: 2,500 - 8,000 SHU

Ingredients
- 8 fresh jalapeño peppers, stemmed and chopped
- 3 cloves garlic, minced
- 1/2 cup fresh lime juice
- 1/4 cup white vinegar
- 1 tablespoon honey
- 1 teaspoon salt
- 1/4 cup chopped fresh cilantro
- 1/2 cup water

Instructions
1. *Preparation:*
   - Remove the stems and chop the peppers. Mince the garlic and chop the cilantro.
2. *Blending:*
   - Combine the chopped jalapeño peppers, garlic, lime juice, white vinegar, honey, salt, cilantro, and water in a blender.
   - Blend until smooth. If the sauce is too thick, add more water a tablespoon at a time until the desired consistency is reached.
3. *Straining (Optional)*

The sauce can be kept refrigerated for several months.

Nutritional Information (per tablespoon): Calories: 7, Total Fat: 0g, Sodium: 85mg, Total Carbohydrates: 1.5g, Sugars: 0.5g, Protein: 0g

Tips
- This fresh and zesty sauce pairs well with grilled chicken, fish tacos, and as a dipping sauce for chips.
- For an added twist, try adding a small amount of fresh mint to the blender for a unique flavor profile.

7: FRESH LEMON ZEST AND ANAHEIM PEPPER HOT SAUCE

Yield: Approximately 2 cups	Prep Time: 15 minutes	Scoville: 500 - 2,500 SHU

Ingredients

- 6 Anaheim peppers, stemmed and chopped
- Zest of 2 lemons
- Juice of 2 lemons
- 1/2 medium onion, chopped
- 3 cloves garlic, minced
- 1/4 cup apple cider vinegar
- 1 tablespoon honey
- 1 teaspoon salt
- 1/4 cup water
- 1/4 cup fresh parsley, chopped

Instructions

1. *Preparation:*
   - Remove the stems and chop the peppers. Zest and juice the lemons. Chop the onion and parsley, and mince the garlic.
2. *Mixing:*
   - In a large mixing bowl, combine the chopped Anaheim peppers, lemon zest, lemon juice, onion, garlic, apple cider vinegar, honey, salt, water, and chopped parsley.
   - Stir the mixture thoroughly to ensure all ingredients are well combined.

The sauce can be kept refrigerated for several weeks.

Nutritional Information (per tablespoon): Calories: 5, Total Fat: 0g, Sodium: 85mg, Total Carbohydrates: 1g, Sugars: 0.5g, Protein: 0g

Tips

- This sauce pairs well with seafood, grilled chicken, and as a dressing for salads.
- For an added depth of flavor, try adding a teaspoon of fresh dill or mint during the mixing process.
- Since this is a fresh, uncooked sauce, it should be consumed relatively quickly or kept refrigerated to maintain its freshness.

8: PINEAPPLE-GINGER HOT SAUCE WITH BASIL

Yield: Approximately 1.5 cups	Prep Time: 15 minutes	Scoville: 50,000 - 100,000 SHU

Ingredients

- 1 cup fresh pineapple, finely chopped
- 3 fresh Thai bird's eye chilies
- 1/4 cup fresh basil leaves, packed
- 1-inch piece of fresh ginger, peeled and minced
- 2 cloves garlic, minced
- 1/4 cup fresh lime juice
- 2 tablespoons rice vinegar
- 1 tablespoon honey (optional for added sweetness)
- 1/2 teaspoon salt

Instructions

1. *Preparation of Ingredients:*
   - Finely chop the fresh pineapple and mince the ginger and garlic.
   - Wear gloves to handle the Thai bird's eye chilies, removing the stems and seeds before chopping.
2. *Blending:*
   - In a high-speed blender combine the chopped pineapple, Thai bird's eye chilies, fresh basil leaves, minced ginger, minced garlic, lime juice, rice vinegar, honey (if using), and salt.
   - Blend the mixture on high until smooth. The fresh pineapple and basil will add a unique tropical flavor, while the ginger and chilies bring heat and complexity.
3. *Adjusting Consistency:*
   - If the sauce is too thick, add a little more lime juice or rice vinegar until you reach your desired consistency. The result should be a smooth, pourable sauce with a vibrant color.
4. *Tasting and Adjusting:*
   - Taste the sauce and adjust the seasoning as needed. Add more salt, lime juice, or honey to adjust the flavors to your preference.

Store in the refrigerator, where it will stay fresh for up to two weeks.

Nutritional Information (per tablespoon): Calories: 8, Total Fat: 0g, Sodium: 60mg, Total Carbohydrates: 2g, Sugars: 1.5g, Protein: 0g

Tips

- This sauce pairs beautifully with grilled seafood, chicken, or even drizzled over salads or tropical fruit bowls.

9: ROASTED RED BELL PEPPER AND CAYENNE HOT SAUCE

Yield: Approximately 2 cups	Prep Time: 10 minutes	Scoville: 30,000 - 50,000 SHU

Ingredients

- 2 roasted red bell peppers (store-bought or pre-roaste)
- 6 fresh cayenne peppers, stemmed and chopped
- 1/2 medium onion, chopped
- 3 cloves garlic, minced
- 1/2 cup apple cider vinegar
- 1/4 cup water
- 1 teaspoon salt
- 1 tablespoon sugar

Instructions

1. *Preparation of Ingredients:*
   - If using store-bought roasted red bell peppers, drain them and chop roughly. If you have pre-roasted your own peppers, chop them as well.
   - Stem and chop the cayenne peppers. Chop the onion and mince the garlic cloves.
2. *Blending:*
   - In a high-speed blender or food processor, combine the roasted red bell peppers, chopped cayenne peppers, onion, garlic, apple cider vinegar, water, salt, and sugar.
   - Blend on high until the mixture is smooth. The roasted red bell peppers will add a sweet, smoky flavor, while the cayenne peppers bring heat and spice.
3. *Adjusting Consistency:*
   - If the sauce is too thick, add more water a tablespoon at a time until you reach the desired consistency. The sauce should be smooth and pourable.
4. *Tasting and Adjusting:*
   - Taste the sauce and adjust the seasoning as needed. Add more salt, vinegar, or sugar to balance the flavors according to your preference.

Store in the refrigerator, where it will stay fresh for up to two weeks.

Nutritional Information (per tablespoon): Calories: 10, Total Fat: 0g, Sodium: 90mg, Total Carbohydrates: 2g, Sugars: 1g, Protein: 0g

Tips

- This quick and easy hot sauce is perfect for adding a fiery kick to grilled meats, roasted vegetables, and barbecue dishes.
- Using pre-roasted red bell peppers saves time and still provides the smoky, sweet depth of flavor that complements the heat of the cayenne peppers.

10: FRESH SPICY GUAJILLO PEPPER HOT SAUCE

Yield: Approximately 1.5 cups	Prep Time: 20 minutes (includes soaking time)	Scoville: 100,000 - 350,000 SHU

Ingredients

- 8 dried Guajillo peppers, seeds removed and soaked in warm water
- 4 fresh habanero peppers, stemmed and seeded
- 3 cloves garlic, minced
- 1/4 cup apple cider vinegar
- 1/4 cup fresh lime juice
- 2 tablespoons olive oil
- 1 teaspoon salt
- 1/2 teaspoon smoked paprika
- 1/4 teaspoon ground cumin

Instructions

1. *Preparing the Guajillo Peppers:*
   - Remove the stems and seeds from the dried Guajillo peppers.
   - Place the peppers in a bowl and cover them with warm water. Let them soak for about 10 minutes until they soften.
2. *Blending:*
   - Drain the soaked Guajillo peppers and add them to a high-speed blender or food processor.
   - Add the fresh habanero peppers, minced garlic, apple cider vinegar, lime juice, olive oil, salt, smoked paprika, and ground cumin to the blender.
3. *Blending Until Smooth:*
   - Blend the mixture on high until smooth. The combination of the soaked Guajillo peppers and fresh habaneros will create a sauce with a deep, spicy flavor and a rich, smooth texture.
4. *Tasting and Adjusting:*
   - Taste the sauce and adjust the seasoning if necessary. You can add more salt, lime juice, or even an extra habanero if you want to turn up the heat further.

Store in the refrigerator, where it will keep fresh for up to two weeks.

Nutritional Information (per tablespoon): Calories: 10, Total Fat: 1g, Sodium: 90mg, Total Carbohydrates: 1g, Sugars: 0g, Protein: 0g

Tips

- The use of both dried and fresh peppers adds layers of flavor that make this sauce stand out, offering a rich, deep heat with a bright finish from the lime juice.

11: FRESH HABANERO-CARROT HOT SAUCE

Yield: 2 cups   **Prep Time: 20 minutes**   **Scoville: 100,000 - 350,000 SHU**

Ingredients

- 10 habanero peppers, stemmed and seeded
- 2 medium carrots, peeled and finely grated
- 1 medium onion, finely chopped
- 4 cloves garlic, minced
- 1/2 cup distilled white vinegar
- 1/4 cup lime juice (freshly squeezed)
- 1/4 cup water
- 1 teaspoon salt
- 1 tablespoon honey (optional for sweetness)
- Zest of 1 lime

Instructions

1. *Preparation of Ingredients:*
   - Finely grate the carrots and chop the onion and garlic. Stem and seed the habanero peppers, then roughly chop them.
   - Combine the chopped habanero peppers, grated carrots, chopped onion, minced garlic, lime zest, and salt in a large mixing bowl.
2. *Blending:*
   - In a high-speed blender, combine the prepared vegetable mixture with the distilled white vinegar, lime juice, and water.
   - Blend the mixture on high until smooth. The honey can be added during this step if you prefer a touch of sweetness to balance the heat.
   - If the sauce is too thick, add additional water or vinegar a little at a time until the desired consistency is reached.
3. *Straining (Optional)*

The hot sauce can be stored for several months when kept refrigerated.

Nutritional Information (per tablespoon): Calories: 5, Total Fat: 0g, Sodium: 95mg, Total Carbohydrates: 1g, Sugars: 0.5g, Protein: 0g

Tips

- This sauce is excellent for drizzling over salads, grilled vegetables, or as a dip for chips. The raw carrots add a subtle sweetness that balances the fiery habaneros.
- For added complexity, consider adding fresh herbs like cilantro or parsley during blending.

12: SPICY CHILI OIL

Yield: 1 cup

Prep time: 5 min
Cook time: 10 min

Scoville: 30,000 - 50,000 SHU

Ingredients
- 1 cup olive oil
- 6 dried red chili peppers (like arbol or Thai), crushed
- 1 tablespoon red pepper flakes
- 4 cloves garlic, sliced
- 1 teaspoon Sichuan peppercorns (optional)
- 1 teaspoon smoked paprika
- 1/2 teaspoon salt

Instructions
1. *Infusing Oil:*
   - Heat olive oil in a small saucepan over low heat.
   - Add crushed dried chili peppers, red pepper flakes, garlic slices, Sichuan peppercorns (if using), smoked paprika, and salt.
   - Simmer on low heat for about 10 minutes, stirring occasionally, until the garlic is golden and the oil is infused with chili flavor.
2. *Cooling and Straining:*
   - Remove the saucepan from heat and let the oil cool completely. Strain the oil through a fine-mesh strainer into a clean, sterilized bottle.

The oil can be kept for up to a month in a cool dark place.

Nutritional Information (per tablespoon): Calories: 120, Total Fat: 14g, Sodium: 40mg, Total Carbohydrates: 0g, Sugars: 0g, Protein: 0g

Tips
- Use this spicy oil for drizzling over pizza, pasta, grilled vegetables, or as a base for stir-fries.
- Ensure the garlic doesn't burn, as this can impart a bitter taste to the oil.

13: MANGO-HABANERO HOT SAUCE

Yield: 2 cups

Prep Time: 15 minutes
Cook Time: 30 minutes
(including roasting time)

Scoville: 100,000 - 350,000 SHU

Ingredients
- 6 habanero peppers
- 1 ripe mango, peeled and chopped
- 1/2 medium onion, chopped
- 3 cloves garlic, minced
- 1/2 cup white vinegar
- 1/2 cup water
- 1 teaspoon salt
- 1 tablespoon honey
- Juice of 1 lime

Instructions

1. Preparation
- o Remove the stems and seeds. Peel and chop the mango. Chop the onion and mince the garlic.

2. Roasting
- o Preheat your oven to 400°F.
- o Place the habanero peppers and chopped mango on a baking sheet lined with parchment paper.
- o Roast in the oven for 15 minutes, turning halfway through, until the peppers and mango are slightly charred and soft.

3. Cooking
- o In a medium saucepan, heat a small amount of oil over medium heat. Add the chopped onion and garlic and sauté for 3-4 minutes until softened.
- o Add the roasted habanero peppers, mango, vinegar, and water to the saucepan.
- o Bring the mixture to a boil, then reduce the heat to low and let it simmer for about 10 minutes.

4. Blending
- o Remove the saucepan from the heat and allow the mixture to cool slightly.
- o Transfer the mixture to a blender. Add the salt, honey, and lime juice. Blend until smooth. If the sauce is too thick, add more water a little at a time until you reach the desired consistency.

5. Straining

- o For a smoother texture, pour the blended mixture through a fine-mesh strainer into a bowl, pressing down with a spoon to extract as much liquid as possible.

Nutritional Information (per tablespoon):   Calories: 10, Total Fat: 0g, Sodium: 90mg, Total Carbohydrates: 2g, Sugars: 1g, Protein: 0g

Tips

- For a sweeter sauce, increase the amount of honey or use a slightly overripe mango.
- This sauce pairs well with grilled fish, chicken, and as a dipping sauce for fried appetizers.
- Ensure the roasted peppers and mango have a nice char, as this adds a depth of flavor to the sauce.

14: SERRANO-PINEAPPLE HOT SAUCE

Yield: 1.5 cups   **Prep Time: 10 minutes**   **Scoville: 20,000 - 30,000 SHU**

Ingredients

- 8 serrano peppers, stemmed and chopped
- 1 cup fresh pineapple, finely chopped
- 2 cloves garlic, minced
- 1/4 cup apple cider vinegar
- 1/4 cup fresh lime juice
- 2 tablespoons honey
- 1 teaspoon salt
- 1/2 teaspoon ground cumin

Instructions

1. *Preparation of Ingredients:*
   - Stem and chop the serrano peppers. You can leave the seeds in for extra heat. Finely chop the fresh pineapple and mince the garlic cloves.
2. *Blending:*
   - In a high-speed blender or food processor, mix the chopped serrano peppers, pineapple, minced garlic, apple cider vinegar, lime juice, honey, salt, and ground cumin.
   - Blend on high until the mixture is smooth. The pineapple will add a sweet contrast to the fiery serrano peppers, while the vinegar and lime juice provide acidity.
3. *Adjusting Consistency:*
   - If the sauce is too thick, incorporate a small amount of water or extra lime juice to achieve your desired consistency. The sauce should be smooth and slightly thick.
4. *Tasting and Adjusting:*
   - Taste the sauce and adjust the seasoning if necessary. Add more salt, honey, or lime juice to balance the flavors to your liking.

Store in the refrigerator, where it will stay fresh for up to two weeks.

Nutritional Information (per tablespoon): Calories: 12, Total Fat: 0g, Sodium: 100mg, Total Carbohydrates: 3g, Sugars: 2g, Protein: 0g

Tips

- The combination of serrano peppers and pineapple provides a unique balance of sweet and spicy, making it an excellent addition to grilled meats, tacos, or even as a tropical dip.

15: ROASTED ANAHEIM AND TOMATILLO HOT SAUCE

Yield: 2 cups

Prep Time: 15 minutes
Cook time: 20 minutes

Scoville: 500 - 2,500 SHU

Ingredients

- 6 Anaheim peppers, stemmed and chopped
- 4 medium tomatillos, husked and chopped
- 1/2 medium onion, chopped
- 3 cloves garlic, minced
- 1/2 cup apple cider vinegar
- 1/4 cup lime juice
- 1 tablespoon honey
- 1 teaspoon salt
- 1/4 cup water

Instructions

1. *Roasting Peppers and Tomatillos:*
   - Preheat your oven to 425°F (220°C).
   - Arrange the Anaheim peppers and tomatillos on a baking sheet. Roast for about 15-20 minutes, turning occasionally, until the skins are charred and blistered.
   - Remove from the oven and place in a bowl covered with plastic wrap for 10 minutes.
   - Peel the skins off the peppers, remove the stems and seeds, and chop the peppers. Chop the roasted tomatillos.

2. *Sautéing:*
   - In a large saucepan, heat a small amount of oil over medium heat. Add the chopped onion and minced garlic and sauté for about 5 minutes until the onion is translucent and the garlic is fragrant.

3. *Combining Ingredients:*
   - Add the chopped roasted Anaheim peppers, tomatillos, apple cider vinegar, lime juice, honey, salt, and water to the saucepan.
   - Bring the mixture to a boil, then reduce the heat to low and let it simmer for about 10 minutes.

4. *Blending:*
   - Allow the mixture to cool slightly before transferring it to a blender.
   - Blend until smooth.

5. *Straining (Optional)*
   - The sauce can be kept refrigerated for several months.

Nutritional Information (per tablespoon): Calories: 9, Total Fat: 0g, Sodium: 85mg, Total Carbohydrates: 2g, Sugars: 0.5g, Protein: 0g

16: FRESNO PEPPER AND GARLIC HOT SAUCE

Yield: 2 cups	Prep Time: 15 minutes	Scoville: 2,500 - 10,000
	Cook Time: 15 minutes	SHU

Ingredients

- 10 Fresno peppers, stemmed and chopped
- 1/2 medium onion, chopped
- 6 cloves garlic, minced
- 1/2 cup white vinegar
- 1/4 cup lemon juice
- 1 tablespoon honey
- 1 teaspoon salt
- 1/4 cup water

Instructions

1. *Preparation:*
   - Remove the stems and chop the peppers. Chop the onion and mince the garlic.
2. *Cooking:*
   - In a medium saucepan, combine the chopped Fresno peppers, onion, garlic, vinegar, lemon juice, honey, salt, and water.
   - Bring the mixture to a boil over medium-high heat. Reduce the heat to low and let it simmer for about 15 minutes, or until the ingredients are soft.
3. *Blending:*
   - Allow the mixture to cool slightly before transferring it to a blender.
   - Blend until smooth. If the sauce is too thick, add more water a tablespoon at a time until the desired consistency is reached.
4. *Straining (Optional)*

The sauce can be kept refrigerated for several months.

Nutritional Information (per tablespoon): Calories: 8, Total Fat: 0g, Sodium: 85mg, Total Carbohydrates: 1.5g, Sugars: 0.5g, Protein: 0g

Tips

- This sauce pairs well with grilled meats, roasted vegetables, and as a condiment for sandwiches.
- For an added depth of flavor, try roasting the garlic before adding it to the saucepan.

17: HOMEMADE SRIRACHA MAYONNAISE

Yield: 1 cup	Prep Time: 10 minutes	Scoville: 2,500 - 5,000 SHU

Ingredients

- 1 large egg yolk
- 1 teaspoon Dijon mustard
- 1 tablespoon lemon juice
- 1 cup neutral oil (like canola or grapeseed)
- 2 tablespoons Sriracha sauce
- 1/2 teaspoon garlic powder
- 1/2 teaspoon honey (optional)
- 1/4 teaspoon salt
- 1/4 teaspoon black pepper

Instructions

1. *Starting the Emulsion:*
   - In a medium bowl, whisk together the egg yolk, Dijon mustard, and lemon juice until well combined.
2. *Adding the Oil:*
   - Begin adding the oil very slowly, just a few drops at a time, while whisking continuously. Once the mixture starts to thicken, you can add the oil in a thin, steady stream. Continue whisking until all the oil is incorporated and the mixture is thick and creamy.
3. *Mixing in Flavors:*
   - Stir in the Sriracha sauce, garlic powder, honey (if using), salt, and black pepper. Mix until everything is well combined and smooth.
4. *Adjusting:*
   - Taste the Sriracha mayonnaise and adjust the seasoning if needed. You can add more Sriracha for extra heat or more lemon juice for extra tang.

The mayonnaise can be kept refrigerated for up to a week.

Nutritional Information (per tablespoon): Calories: 100, Total Fat: 11g, Sodium: 100mg, Total Carbohydrates: 0g, Sugars: 0g, Protein: 0g

Tips

- Make sure to add the oil very slowly at first to ensure the mayonnaise emulsifies properly.
- Freshly made mayonnaise has a more delicate flavor than store-bought, so adjust the seasoning to your taste.

18: CUCUMBER-THAI CHILI HOT SAUCE

Yield: 2 cups

Prep Time: 15 minutes
Cook Time: 10 minutes

Scoville: 50,000 - 100,000 SHU

Ingredients

- 2 cucumbers, peeled and chopped
- 6 Thai bird's eye chilies, stemmed and chopped
- 1/2 medium onion, chopped
- 3 cloves garlic, minced
- 1/2 cup white vinegar
- 1/4 cup lime juice
- 1 tablespoon honey
- 1 teaspoon salt
- 1/4 cup fresh cilantro, chopped
- 1 teaspoon ground coriander

Instructions

1. *Preparation:*
   - Remove the stems and chop the chilies. Peel and chop the cucumbers, and mince the garlic. Chop the onion and cilantro.
2. *Cooking:*
   - In a medium saucepan, combine the chopped cucumbers, Thai chilies, onion, garlic, vinegar, lime juice, honey, salt, and ground coriander.
   - Bring the mixture to a boil over medium-high heat. Reduce the heat to low and let it simmer for about 10 minutes, or until the ingredients are soft.
3. *Blending:*
   - Allow the mixture to cool slightly before transferring it to a blender.
   - Add the chopped cilantro and blend until smooth. If the sauce is too thick, add more water a tablespoon at a time until the desired consistency is reached.
4. *Straining (Optional)*

The sauce can be kept refrigerated for several months.

Nutritional Information (per tablespoon): Calories: 7, Total Fat: 0g, Sodium: 85mg, Total Carbohydrates: 1.5g, Sugars: 0.5g, Protein: 0g

Tips

- Make sure to use fresh, high-quality cucumbers.
- This sauce pairs well with seafood, grilled chicken, and as a salad dressing.
- Consider adding a teaspoon of ground coriander.

19: SPICY CHICKPEA AND RED PEPPER HOT SAUCE

Yield: 2 cups

Prep Time: 15 minutes
Cook Time: 20 minutes

Scoville: 10,000 - 23,000 SHU

Ingredients

- 1 can (15 oz) chickpeas, drained and rinsed
- 4 red bell peppers, roasted and chopped
- 4 serrano peppers, stemmed and chopped
- 1/2 medium onion, chopped
- 3 cloves garlic, minced
- 1/2 cup apple cider vinegar
- 1/4 cup lemon juice
- 1 tablespoon honey
- 1 teaspoon salt
- 1 teaspoon ground cumin

Instructions

1. *Roasting Peppers:*
   - Preheat your oven to 425°F (220°C).
   - Place the red bell peppers on a baking sheet and roast for about 15-20 minutes.
   - Remove from the oven and place in a bowl covered with plastic wrap for 10 minutes. Peel off the skins, remove the stems and seeds, and chop the peppers.

2. *Preparation:*
   - Remove the stems and chop the peppers. Chop the onion and mince the garlic.

3. *Cooking:*
   - In a medium saucepan, combine the chickpeas, chopped red bell peppers, serrano peppers, onion, garlic, vinegar, lemon juice, honey, salt, and ground cumin.
   - Bring the mixture to a boil over medium-high heat. Reduce the heat to low and let it simmer for about 10-15 minutes, or until the ingredients are soft.

4. *Blending:*
   - Allow the mixture to cool slightly before transferring it to a blender.
   - Blend until smooth. If the sauce is too thick, add more water a tablespoon at a time until the desired consistency is reached.

5. *Straining (Optional)*

The sauce can be kept refrigerated for several months.

Nutritional Information (per tablespoon): Calories: 15, Total Fat: 0g, Sodium: 85mg, Total Carbohydrates: 3g, Sugars: 1g, Protein: 1g

20: ROASTED POBLANO AND SERRANO HOT SAUCE

Yield: 2 cups	Prep Time: 15 minutes	Scoville: 10,000 - 23,000
	Cook Time: 25 minutes	SHU
	Fermentation Time:	
	5 days	

Ingredients

- 4 poblano peppers, roasted
- 4 serrano peppers, stemmed and chopped
- 1/2 medium onion, chopped
- 3 cloves garlic, minced
- 1/2 cup white vinegar
- 1/4 cup lemon juice
- 1 tablespoon honey
- 1 teaspoon salt
- 1/4 cup water
- 1 teaspoon ground cumin

Instructions

1. *Roasting Peppers:*
   - Preheat your oven to 425°F (220°C).
   - Place the poblano peppers on a baking sheet and roast for about 15-20 minutes, turning occasionally, until the skins are charred and blistered.
   - Remove from the oven and place in a bowl covered with plastic wrap for 10 minutes. Peel off the skins, remove the stems and seeds, and chop the peppers.
2. Preparation:
   - Remove the stems and chop the peppers. Chop the onion and mince the garlic.
3. *Cooking:*
   - In a medium saucepan, combine the chopped poblano peppers, serrano peppers, onion, garlic, vinegar, lemon juice, honey, salt, water, and ground cumin.
   - Bring the mixture to a boil over medium-high heat. Reduce the heat to low and let it simmer for about 10-15 minutes, or until the ingredients are soft.
4. *Blending:*
   - Allow the mixture to cool slightly before transferring it to a blender.
   - Blend until smooth. If the sauce is too thick, add more water a tablespoon at a time until the desired consistency is reached.
5. *Straining (Optional)*
6. *Fermentation (Optional)*

The sauce can be kept refrigerated for several months.

Nutritional Information (per tablespoon): Calories: 10, Total Fat: 0g, Sodium: 85mg, Total Carbohydrates: 2g, Sugars: 1g, Protein: 0g

Tips

- For a milder sauce, reduce the number of serrano peppers or substitute with milder varieties like jalapeños.
- This sauce pairs well with grilled meats, roasted vegetables, and as a topping for tacos and sandwiches.

21: CINNAMON HABANERO HOT SAUCE

Yield: 2 cups   **Prep Time: 15 minutes**   **Scoville: 100,000 - 350,000**
                         Cook time: 15 minutes   **SHU**

Ingredients

- 6 habanero peppers
- 1/2 medium onion, chopped
- 1/2 cup apple cider vinegar
- 1/4 cup lime juice
- 1 tablespoon honey
- 1 teaspoon salt
- 1 teaspoon ground cinnamon
- 1/4 teaspoon ground allspice
- 1/2 cup water

Instructions

1. *Preparation:*
   - Remove the stems and chop the peppers. Chop the onion.
2. *Cooking:*
   - In a medium saucepan, combine the chopped habanero peppers, onion, apple cider vinegar, lime juice, honey, salt, ground cinnamon, ground allspice, and water.
   - Bring the mixture to a boil over medium-high heat. Reduce the heat to low and let it simmer for about 15 minutes.
3. *Blending:*
   - Allow the mixture to cool slightly before transferring it to a blender.
   - Blend until smooth. If the sauce is too thick, add more water a tablespoon at a time until the desired consistency is reached.
4. *Straining (Optional)*

The sauce can be kept refrigerated for several months.

Nutritional Information (per tablespoon): Calories: 10, Total Fat: 0g, Sodium: 90mg, Total Carbohydrates: 2g, Sugars: 1g, Protein: 0g

Tips

- This sauce pairs well with roasted meats, sweet potatoes, and as a glaze for grilled chicken or pork.
- For an added depth of flavor, try adding a small amount of roasted butternut squash or pumpkin puree during the blending process.

22: ROASTED RED BERRY HABANERO HOT SAUCE

Yield: 2 cups	Prep Time: 15 minutes	Scoville: 100,000 - 350,000
	Cook Time: 20 minutes	SHU

Ingredients

- 6 habanero peppers, stemmed and chopped
- 1 cup strawberries, hulled and halved
- 1 cup raspberries
- 1/2 medium red onion, chopped
- 1/2 cup apple cider vinegar
- 1/4 cup lime juice
- 1 tablespoon honey
- 1 teaspoon salt

Instructions

1. *Roasting Ingredients:*
   - Preheat your oven to 425°F (220°C).
   - Place the habanero peppers, strawberries, raspberries, red onion on a baking sheet.
   - Roast for about 15-20 minutes, turning occasionally, until the ingredients are soft and slightly charred.
   - Remove from the oven and let cool.
2. *Preparation:*
   - Chop the roasted habanero peppers and red onion if not already done.
3. *Cooking:*
   - In a medium saucepan, combine the roasted habanero peppers, strawberries, raspberries, red onion, apple cider vinegar, lime juice, honey, and salt.
   - Bring the mixture to a boil over medium-high heat. Reduce the heat to low and let it simmer for about 5 minutes.
4. *Blending:*
   - Allow the mixture to cool slightly before transferring it to a blender.
   - Blend until smooth.
5. *Straining (Optional)*

The sauce can be kept refrigerated for several months.

Nutritional Information (per tablespoon): Calories: 12, Total Fat: 0g, Sodium: 85mg, Total Carbohydrates: 3g, Sugars: 2g, Protein: 0g

Tips

- This sauce pairs well with grilled meats, cheese platters, and as a topping for desserts like cheesecake or ice cream. For an added depth of flavor, try adding a splash of balsamic vinegar.

23: BALSAMIC CHIPOTLE HOT SAUCE

Yield: 2 cups

Prep Time: 15 minutes
Cook Time: 15 minutes
Fermentation Time: 5 days (optional)

Scoville: 2,500 - 8,000 SHU

Ingredients

- 6 chipotle peppers in adobo sauce, chopped
- 1/2 cup balsamic vinegar
- 1/2 medium red onion, chopped
- 3 cloves garlic, minced
- 1/4 cup lime juice
- 1 tablespoon honey
- 1 teaspoon salt
- 1/2 teaspoon smoked paprika
- 1/4 cup water

Instructions

1. *Preparation:*
   - Chop the chipotle peppers in adobo sauce. Chop the red onion and mince the garlic.
2. *Cooking:*
   - In a medium saucepan, combine the chopped chipotle peppers, balsamic vinegar, red onion, garlic, lime juice, honey, salt, smoked paprika, and water.
   - Bring the mixture to a boil over medium-high heat. Reduce the heat to low and let it simmer for about 15 minutes, or until the ingredients are soft.
3. *Blending:*
   - Allow the mixture to cool slightly before transferring it to a blender.
   - Blend until smooth. If the sauce is too thick, add more water a tablespoon at a time until the desired consistency is reached.
4. *Straining (Optional)*
5. *Fermentation (Optional)*

The sauce can be kept refrigerated for several months.

Nutritional Information (per tablespoon): Calories: 10 ,Total Fat: 0g, Sodium: 90mg, Total Carbohydrates: 2g, Sugars: 1g, Protein: 0g

Tips

- This sauce pairs well with grilled meats, roasted vegetables, and as a marinade for chicken or steak.
- For an added depth of flavor, try adding a small amount of roasted garlic.

24: GRILLED GREEN ZUCCHINI AND SERRANO HOT SAUCE

Yield: 2 cups

Prep Time: 20 minutes
Cook Time: 20 minutes

Scoville: 10,000 - 23,000 SHU

Ingredients

- 3 medium zucchinis, sliced
- 6 serrano peppers, stemmed and chopped
- 1/2 medium green bell pepper, chopped
- 1/2 medium onion, chopped
- 3 cloves garlic, minced
- 1/2 cup apple cider vinegar
- 1/4 cup lime juice
- 1 tablespoon honey
- 1 teaspoon salt

Instructions

1. *Grilling Zucchini and Serrano Peppers:*
   - Preheat your grill to medium-high heat.
   - Slice the zucchinis into 1/4-inch thick rounds.
   - Place the zucchini slices and whole serrano peppers on the grill.
   - Grill for about 5-7 minutes on each side, until they are tender and have nice grill marks. Remove from the grill and let cool slightly.
   - Chop the grilled serrano peppers.
2. *Preparation:*
   - Chop the grilled zucchini and green bell pepper. Finely chop the onion and mince the garlic.
3. *Cooking:*
   - In a large saucepan, combine the grilled zucchini, chopped serrano peppers, green bell pepper, onion, garlic, vinegar, lime juice, honey, and salt.
   - Bring the mixture to a boil over medium-high heat. Reduce the heat to low and let it simmer for about 10 minutes, stirring occasionally.

Nutritional Information (per tablespoon): Calories: 8, Total Fat: 0g, Sodium: 85mg, Total Carbohydrates: 1.5g, Sugars: 0.5g, Protein: 0g

Tips

- This green sauce pairs well with grilled chicken, fish, and as a dressing for salads.
- For an added depth of flavor, try adding a teaspoon of ground cumin or fresh chopped herbs like cilantro or parsley.

25: CHUNKY ROASTED RED PEPPER AND HABANERO HOT SAUCE

Yield: 2 cups	Prep Time: 20 minutes	Scoville: 100,000 - 350,000
	Cook Time: 20 minutes	SHU
	Fermentation Time: 5 days (optional)	

Ingredients

- 4 habanero peppers, stemmed and finely chopped
- 4 red bell peppers, roasted, peeled, and chopped
- 1/2 medium red onion, finely chopped
- 3 cloves garlic, minced
- 1/2 cup apple cider vinegar
- 1/4 cup lime juice
- 1 tablespoon honey
- 1 teaspoon salt
- 1 teaspoon smoked paprika
- 1 medium tomato, finely chopped

Instructions

1. *Roasting Peppers:*
   - Preheat your oven to 425°F (220°C).
   - Place the red bell peppers on a baking sheet and roast for about 15-20 minutes, turning occasionally.
   - Remove from the oven and place in a bowl covered with plastic wrap for 10 minutes. Peel off the skins, remove the stems and seeds, and chop the peppers.
2. *Preparation:*
   - Remove the stems and finely chop the habaneros. Finely chop the red onion and tomato, and mince the garlic.
3. *Cooking:*
   - In a large saucepan, combine the chopped habanero peppers, roasted red bell peppers, red onion, garlic, vinegar, lime juice, honey, salt, and smoked paprika.
   - Bring the mixture to a boil over medium-high heat. Reduce the heat to low and let it simmer for about 15 minutes, stirring occasionally.
4. *Adding the Tomato:*
   - Add the finely chopped tomato to the saucepan and simmer for an additional 5 minutes, stirring occasionally to ensure even cooking.
5. *Cooling and Fermentation (Optional):*
   - Allow the mixture to cool slightly. For deeper flavors, pour the mixture into a clean glass jar with an airlock lid.

○ Let the sauce ferment at room temperature for about 5 days, stirring daily.
The sauce can be kept refrigerated for several months.

Nutritional Information (per tablespoon): Calories: 10, Total Fat: 0g, Sodium: 85mg, Total Carbohydrates: 2g, Sugars: 1g, Protein: 0g

Tips
- This chunky sauce pairs well with grilled meats, roasted vegetables, and as a topping for burgers and sandwiches.
- For an added depth of flavor, try adding a teaspoon of ground cumin or fresh chopped herbs like cilantro or parsley.

26: INFERNO GHOST PEPPER HOT SAUCE

Yield: 2 cups   **Prep Time: 15 minutes**   **Scoville: 855,000 –**
Cook Time: 15 minutes   **1,041,427 SHU**
Fermentation Time: 5
days (optional)

Ingredients

- 6 ghost peppers (Bhut Jolokia), stemmed and chopped
- 2 habanero peppers, stemmed and chopped
- 1/2 medium onion, chopped
- 3 cloves garlic, minced
- 1/2 cup white vinegar
- 1/4 cup lime juice
- 1 tablespoon honey
- 1 teaspoon salt
- 1/4 cup water

Instructions

1. *Preparation:*
   - Remove the stems and chop the peppers. Chop the onion and mince the garlic.
2. *Cooking:*
   - In a medium saucepan, combine the chopped ghost peppers, habanero peppers, onion, garlic, vinegar, lime juice, honey, salt, and water.
   - Bring the mixture to a boil over medium-high heat. Reduce the heat to low and let it simmer for about 15 minutes, or until the ingredients are soft.
3. *Blending:*
   - Allow the mixture to cool slightly before transferring it to a blender.
   - Blend until smooth. If the sauce is too thick, add more water a tablespoon at a time until the desired consistency is reached.
4. *Straining (Optional)*
5. *Fermentation (Optional):*
   - To develop deeper flavors, pour the strained sauce into a clean glass jar with an airlock lid.
   - Let the sauce ferment for about 5 days. Check the pH to ensure it remains below 4.6.

Nutritional Information (per tablespoon): Calories: 10, Total Fat: 0g, Sodium: 85mg, Total Carbohydrates: 2g, Sugars: 1g, Protein: 0g

Tips

- This sauce is extremely spicy due to the use of ghost peppers and habanero peppers. Handle with care and start with small amounts when using it.

27: SMOKY POBLANO AND TAMARIND HOT SAUCE

Yield: 1.5 cups	Prep Time: 10 minutes	Scoville: 2,000 - 10,000 SHU

Ingredients

- 4 poblano peppers, stemmed, seeded, and chopped
- 2 serrano peppers, stemmed and chopped (for added heat)
- 2 cloves garlic, minced
- 1/4 cup tamarind paste (available in most grocery stores)
- 1/4 cup apple cider vinegar
- 1 tablespoon soy sauce
- 1 tablespoon honey
- 1 teaspoon smoked paprika
- 1/2 teaspoon ground cumin
- 1/4 teaspoon salt

Instructions

1. *Preparation of Ingredients:*
   - Stem, seed, and chop the poblano peppers. Chop the serrano peppers, leaving the seeds in for extra heat if desired. Mince the garlic cloves.
2. *Blending:*
   - In a high-speed blender or food processor, combine the chopped poblano peppers, serrano peppers, minced garlic, tamarind paste, apple cider vinegar, soy sauce, honey, smoked paprika, ground cumin, and salt.
   - Blend on high until the mixture is smooth. The tamarind adds a tangy and slightly sweet flavor that pairs beautifully with the smoky poblano peppers.
3. *Adjusting Consistency:*
   - If the sauce is too thick, you can add a little more apple cider vinegar or water to reach your desired consistency. The sauce should be smooth and pourable, with a rich, smoky flavor profile.
4. *Tasting and Adjusting:*
   - Taste the sauce and adjust the seasoning if necessary. Add more salt, soy sauce, or honey to balance the flavors to your liking.

Store in the refrigerator, where it will stay fresh for up to two weeks.

Nutritional Information (per tablespoon): Calories: 10, Total Fat: 0g, Sodium: 90mg, Total Carbohydrates: 2g, Sugars: 1g, Protein: 0g

Tips

- This sauce pairs well with grilled meats, roasted vegetables, and even as a unique topping for tacos or enchiladas.

28: SWEET AND TANGY SRIRACHA HOT SAUCE

Yield: 2 cups   **Prep Time: 15 minutes**   **Scoville: 2,500 - 5,000 SHU**
                           Cook time: 15 minutes

Ingredients
- 2 pounds red jalapeño peppers, stemmed and chopped
- 4 cloves garlic, minced
- 1/4 cup light brown sugar
- 1/2 cup white vinegar
- 1/4 cup water
- 1 tablespoon salt
- 1 tablespoon fish sauce (optional)

Instructions

1. Preparation
- Remove the stems and chop the peppers. Mince the garlic.

2. Cooking
- In a large saucepan, combine the chopped jalapeño peppers, minced garlic, light brown sugar, white vinegar, water, and salt.
- Bring the mixture to a boil over medium-high heat. Reduce the heat to low and simmer for about 10-15 minutes, or until the peppers are soft and the sugar has dissolved.

3. Blending
- Allow the mixture to cool slightly before transferring it to a blender.
- Add the fish sauce (if using). Blend until smooth. If the sauce is too thick, add additional water a tablespoon at a time until the desired consistency is reached.

4. Straining (Optional)
The sauce can be kept refrigerated for several months.

Nutritional Information (per tablespoon): Calories: 10, Total Fat: 0g, Sodium: 130mg, Total Carbohydrates: 2g, Sugars: 1.5g, Protein: 0g

Tips
- For a milder sauce, use fewer jalapeño peppers or substitute with Fresno peppers.
- This sweet and tangy Sriracha pairs well with a variety of dishes including noodles, eggs, and grilled meats.

29: FRESH TOMATO AND BELL PEPPER HOT SAUCE

Yield: 2 cups	Prep Time: 15 minutes	Scoville: 2,500 - 8,000 SHU (depending on the jalapeños)

Ingredients

- 3 large tomatoes, chopped
- 1 red bell pepper, chopped
- 1 yellow bell pepper, chopped
- 2 jalapeño peppers, stemmed and chopped
- 1/2 medium red onion, chopped
- 3 cloves garlic, minced
- 1/4 cup apple cider vinegar
- 1/4 cup lime juice
- 1 tablespoon honey
- 1 teaspoon salt

Instructions

1. *Preparation:*
   - Wear kitchen gloves to handle the jalapeño peppers safely. Remove the stems and chop the peppers. Chop the tomatoes, red and yellow bell peppers, red onion, and mince the garlic.
2. *Mixing:*
   - In a large mixing bowl, combine the chopped tomatoes, red bell pepper, yellow bell pepper, jalapeños, red onion, garlic, apple cider vinegar, lime juice, honey, and salt.
   - Stir the mixture thoroughly to ensure all ingredients are well combined.
3. *Blending (Optional)*

The sauce can be kept refrigerated for up to a week.

Nutritional Information (per tablespoon): Calories: 6, Total Fat: 0g, Sodium: 80mg, Total Carbohydrates: 1.2g, Sugars: 0.5g, Protein: 0g

Tips

- For an even milder sauce, you can deseed the jalapeños before chopping them.
- The combination of fresh tomatoes and bell peppers provides a vibrant flavor, making it a great topping for tacos, grilled meats, and salads.
- Since this is a fresh sauce, it should be consumed relatively quickly or kept refrigerated to maintain its freshness.

30: SPICY PEPPERONCINI AND TOMATO HOT SAUCE

Yield: 2 cups	Prep Time: 15 minutes	Scoville: 10,000 - 23,000
	Cook Time: 15 minutes	SHU
	Fermentation Time: 3 days (optional)	

Ingredients

- 10 pepperoncini peppers, stemmed and chopped
- 4 large tomatoes, chopped
- 2 serrano peppers, stemmed and chopped
- 3 cloves garlic, minced
- 1/2 cup white vinegar
- 1/4 cup lemon juice
- 1 tablespoon honey
- 1 teaspoon salt
- 1 teaspoon dried oregano
- 1/4 cup water

Instructions

1. *Preparation:*
   - Remove the stems and chop the pepperoncini and serrano peppers. Chop the tomatoes and red onion, and mince the garlic.
2. *Cooking:*
   - In a medium saucepan, combine the chopped pepperoncini, serrano peppers, tomatoes, garlic, vinegar, lemon juice, honey, salt, oregano, and water.
   - Bring the mixture to a boil over medium-high heat. Reduce the heat to low and let it simmer for about 15 minutes, or until the ingredients are soft.
3. *Blending:*
   - Allow the mixture to cool slightly before transferring it to a blender.
   - Blend until smooth. If the sauce is too thick, add more water a tablespoon at a time until the desired consistency is reached.
4. *Fermentation (Optional)*

The sauce can be kept refrigerated for several weeks.

Nutritional Information (per tablespoon): Calories: 8, Total Fat: 0g, Sodium: 85mg, Total Carbohydrates: 1.5g, Sugars: 0.5g, Protein: 0g

Tips

- Adding a teaspoon of fresh chopped cilantro or parsley during the cooking process can enhance the flavor profile.

31: CREAMY BUTTER AND JALAPEÑO HOT SAUCE

Yield: 1 cup

Prep Time: 10 minutes
Cook Time: 10 minutes

Scoville: 2,500 - 8,000 SHU

Ingredients

- 1/2 cup unsalted butter
- 3 jalapeño peppers, stemmed and finely chopped
- 1/2 cup heavy cream
- 1 tablespoon apple cider vinegar
- 1 tablespoon honey
- 1 teaspoon smoked paprika
- 1/2 teaspoon garlic powder
- 1/2 teaspoon onion powder
- 1/2 teaspoon salt

Instructions

1. *Preparation:*
   - Wear kitchen gloves to handle the jalapeño peppers safely. Remove the stems and finely chop the peppers.
2. *Melting Butter:*
   - In a medium saucepan, melt the unsalted butter over medium heat.
3. *Cooking:*
   - Once the butter is melted, add the finely chopped jalapeño peppers to the saucepan. Cook for about 2-3 minutes until the peppers are softened.
   - Stir in the apple cider vinegar, honey, smoked paprika, garlic powder, onion powder, and salt. Cook for an additional 2 minutes.
4. *Adding Cream:*
   - Reduce the heat to low and slowly stir in the heavy cream.
   - Continue to cook the mixture over low heat, stirring constantly, for about 5 minutes until everything is well combined and heated through.
5. *Blending:*
   - Allow the mixture to cool slightly before transferring it to a blender.
   - Blend until smooth. If the sauce is too thick, add a tablespoon of water at a time until the desired consistency is reached.

Nutritional Information (per tablespoon): Calories: 90, Total Fat: 10g, Sodium: 180mg, Total Carbohydrates: 1g, Sugars: 0.5g, Protein: 0g

Tips

- This creamy butter hot sauce pairs well with grilled chicken, pasta dishes, and as a dipping sauce for breadsticks. The addition of smoked paprika gives the sauce a rich, smoky flavor.

32: FERMENTED PINEAPPLE AND SCOTCH BONNET HOT SAUCE

Yield: 2 cups	Prep Time: 20 minutes	Cook Time: 10 minutes
	Fermentation Time: 7 days	Scoville: 100,000 - 350,000 SHU

Ingredients

- 8 Scotch Bonnet peppers, stemmed and chopped
- 2 cups fresh pineapple, chopped
- 1 medium carrot, grated
- 1/2 medium red onion, chopped
- 4 cloves garlic, minced
- 1/2 cup apple cider vinegar
- 1 tablespoon sea salt
- 1 tablespoon sugar
- 1 cup filtered water

Instructions

1. *Preparation:*
   - Remove the stems and chop the peppers. Chop the pineapple and red onion, grate the carrot, and mince the garlic.
2. *Fermentation Setup:*
   - In a large, sterilized glass jar, combine the Scotch Bonnet peppers, pineapple, carrot, red onion, and garlic.
   - Dissolve the sea salt and sugar in the filtered water. Pour this brine over the vegetables and fruit, making sure they are completely submerged. If needed, use a fermentation weight to keep them submerged.
3. *Fermentation:*
   - Seal the jar with a cheesecloth or fermentation lid to allow gases to escape while keeping contaminants out.
   - Let the mixture ferment at room temperature for 7 days. Check daily to ensure the vegetables and fruit remain submerged and to release any built-up gases.
4. *Cooking:*
   - After 7 days, transfer the fermented mixture to a blender. Add the apple cider vinegar and blend until smooth.
   - Pour the blended mixture into a medium saucepan. Bring to a simmer over medium heat and cook for about 10 minutes, stirring occasionally.
5. *Blending and Straining:*
   - Allow the mixture to cool slightly before transferring it back to the blender. Blend until very smooth.

- For a smoother texture, pour the blended mixture through a fine-mesh strainer into a bowl, pressing down with a spoon to extract as much liquid as possible.

The sauce can be kept refrigerated for several months.

Nutritional Information (per tablespoon): Calories: 8, Total Fat: 0g, Sodium: 85mg, Total Carbohydrates: 2g, Sugars: 1g, Protein: 0g

Tips

- This sauce pairs well with Caribbean dishes, grilled meats, and as a condiment for tropical-themed meals.
- Adding a tablespoon of ginger during fermentation can enhance the flavor profile with a spicy, aromatic note.

33: GRILLED PEPPER & TOMATO HOT SAUCE WITH FRESH HERBS

Yield: 2 cups

Prep Time: 20 minutes
Cook Time: 15 minutes

Scoville: 10,000 - 23,000
SHU

Ingredients

- 8 red and green bell peppers, grilled and chopped
- 3 medium tomatoes, grilled and chopped
- 3 serrano peppers, grilled and chopped
- 1/2 medium red onion, finely chopped
- 4 cloves garlic, minced
- 1/2 cup white wine vinegar
- 1/4 cup lime juice
- 1 teaspoon salt
- 1/4 cup fresh basil, chopped
- 1/4 cup fresh cilantro, chopped

Instructions

1. *Grilling the Peppers and Tomatoes:*
   - Preheat your grill to medium-high heat.
   - Place the red bell peppers, green bell peppers, tomatoes, and serrano peppers on the grill.
   - Grill for about 5-7 minutes on each side until the vegetables are tender and have nice grill marks. Remove from the grill and let cool slightly.
   - Chop the grilled vegetables.
2. *Preparation:*
   - Finely chop the red onion and mince the garlic. Chop the fresh basil and cilantro.
3. *Mixing:*
   - In a large mixing bowl, combine the grilled red bell peppers, green bell peppers, tomatoes, serrano peppers, red onion, garlic, white wine vinegar, lime juice, honey, and salt.
   - Stir the mixture thoroughly to ensure all ingredients are well combined.
4. *Adding Fresh Herbs:*
   - Stir in the chopped basil and cilantro until evenly distributed.

The sauce can be kept refrigerated for up to a month.

Nutritional Information (per tablespoon): Calories: 8, Total Fat: 0g, Sodium: 75mg, Total Carbohydrates: 2g, Sugars: 1g, Protein: 0g

Tips

- This sauce pairs well with grilled meats, roasted vegetables, and as a topping for tacos and sandwiches. Fresh herbs like basil and cilantro add a vibrant, aromatic note.

34: BLACK OLIVE AND ROASTED PEPPER HOT SAUCE

Yield: 2 cups	Prep Time: 20 minutes	Scoville: 10,000 - 23,000
	Cook Time: 20 minutes	SHU
	(including roasting time)	

Ingredients

- 1 cup black olives, pitted and roasted
- 4 poblano peppers, roasted and chopped
- 2 medium tomatoes, roasted and chopped
- 2 serrano peppers, stemmed and chopped
- 1/2 medium red onion, finely chopped
- 3 cloves garlic, minced
- 1/2 cup balsamic vinegar
- 1/4 cup lemon juice
- 1 tablespoon honey
- 1 teaspoon salt

Instructions

1. *Roasting Olives, Peppers, and Tomatoes:*
   - Preheat your oven to 425°F (220°C).
   - Place the black olives, poblano peppers, and tomatoes on a baking sheet.
   - Roast for about 15-20 minutes, turning occasionally, until the peppers and tomatoes are charred and the olives are slightly shriveled. Remove from the oven and let cool slightly.
   - Chop the roasted poblano peppers and tomatoes.
2. *Preparation:*
   - Wear kitchen gloves to handle the serrano peppers safely. Remove the stems and chop the peppers. Finely chop the red onion and mince the garlic.
3. *Blending:*
   - In a blender, combine the black olives, poblano peppers, tomatoes, serrano peppers, red onion, garlic, balsamic vinegar, lemon juice, honey, and salt.
   - Blend until smooth. Add a little water a tablespoon at a time until the desired consistency is reached.

The sauce can be kept refrigerated for up to a month.

Nutritional Information (per tablespoon): Calories: 10, Total Fat: 0g, Sodium: 85mg, Total Carbohydrates: 2g, Sugars: 1g, Protein: 0g

Tips

- Roasting the black olives, peppers, and tomatoes adds a deep, smoky flavor to the sauce. Ensure they are well charred for the best taste.

35: HOMEMADE SRIRACHA SAUCE

Yield: 2 cups

Prep Time: 15 minutes
Fermentation Time: 7 days

Cook time: 10 minutes

Scoville: 2,500 - 8,000 SHU

Ingredients

- 2 pounds red jalapeño peppers, stemmed and chopped
- 1/2 pound red bell peppers, chopped
- 1/4 cup garlic, minced
- 1/4 cup brown sugar
- 1/2 cup white vinegar
- 1/4 cup fish sauce
- 1 tablespoon salt
- 1/4 cup water

Instructions

1. *Preparation:*
   - Remove the stems and chop the red jalapeño and bell peppers. Mince the garlic.
2. *Fermentation Setup:*
   - In a large, sterilized glass jar, combine the chopped red jalapeño peppers, red bell peppers, garlic, brown sugar, and salt.
   - Add water to the jar and mix thoroughly. Ensure the ingredients are fully submerged.
   - Cover the jar with a cheesecloth or fermentation lid to allow gases to escape while keeping contaminants out.
3. *Fermentation:*
   - Let the mixture ferment at room temperature for 7 days. Check daily to ensure the ingredients remain submerged and to release any built-up gases.
4. *Blending:*
   - After 7 days, transfer the fermented mixture to a blender. Add the white vinegar and fish sauce. Blend until smooth.
5. *Cooking:*
   - Pour the blended mixture into a medium saucepan. Bring to a simmer over medium heat and cook for about 10 minutes, stirring occasionally.
6. *Straining:*
   - Allow the mixture to cool slightly before pouring it through a fine-mesh strainer into a bowl, pressing down with a spoon to extract as much liquid as possible.

Nutritional Information (per tablespoon): Calories: 15, Total Fat: 0g, Sodium: 180mg, Total Carbohydrates: 3g, Sugars: 2g, Protein: 0g

36: HOT HONEY SAUCE

Yield: 1.25 cups   **Prep Time: 10 minutes**   **Scoville: 2,500 - 8,000 SHU**
Cook Time: 15 minutes

Ingredients
- 1 cup honey
- 3 Fresno peppers, stemmed and sliced
- 1/4 cup apple cider vinegar
- 2 cloves garlic, minced
- 1 tablespoon lemon juice
- 1/2 teaspoon salt
- 1/4 teaspoon cayenne pepper (optional for extra heat)

Instructions
1. *Preparation:*
   - Remove the stems and slice the peppers.
2. *Cooking:*
   - In a medium saucepan, combine the honey, sliced Fresno peppers, minced garlic, apple cider vinegar, lemon juice, and salt.
   - Bring the mixture to a simmer over medium heat. Reduce the heat to low and let it simmer for about 15 minutes, stirring occasionally to prevent burning.
   - If using, add the cayenne pepper for extra heat.
3. *Cooling:*
   - Remove the saucepan from heat and allow the mixture to cool slightly.
4. *Straining:*

The sauce can be kept for several months in the refrigerator or at room temperature.

Nutritional Information (per tablespoon): Calories: 64, Total Fat: 0g, Sodium: 15mg, Total Carbohydrates: 17g, Sugars: 16g, Protein: 0g

Tips
- This hot honey sauce pairs well with fried chicken, pizza, cheese boards, and as a glaze for roasted vegetables.
- Ensure to stir the sauce frequently while simmering to prevent the honey from burning.
- Store the sauce in a cool, dark place to maintain its flavor and prevent crystallization.

37: SMOKY APRICOT INFERNO SAUCE

Yield: 1.5 cups	Prep Time: 15 minutes	Scoville: 5,000 - 10,000
	Cook Time: 20 minutes	SHU

Ingredients

- 6 dried apricots, chopped
- 4 chipotle peppers in adobo sauce, chopped
- 1/2 cup apple cider vinegar
- 1/4 cup water
- 1 medium onion, chopped
- 1 tablespoon honey
- 1 teaspoon smoked paprika
- 1 teaspoon salt
- 1/2 teaspoon cumin

Instructions

1. *Preparation:*
   - Remove the stems and chop the peppers. Chop the dried apricots, and the onion.
2. *Cooking:*
   - In a medium saucepan, combine the chopped apricots, chipotle peppers, apple cider vinegar, water, onion, honey, smoked paprika, salt, and cumin.
   - Bring the mixture to a boil over medium-high heat. Reduce the heat to low and let it simmer for about 20 minutes, or until the apricots are soft and the flavors are well combined.
3. *Blending:*
   - Allow the mixture to cool slightly before transferring it to a blender.
   - Blend until smooth. Add more water a tablespoon at a time until the desired consistency is reached.
4. *Straining (Optional)*

The sauce can be kept refrigerated for several months.

Nutritional Information (per tablespoon): Calories: 15, Total Fat: 0g, Sodium: 100mg, Total Carbohydrates: 3g, Sugars: 2g, Protein: 0g

Tips

- This sauce can be used as a glaze for tofu, pork or chicken for a deliciously smoky and sweet flavor.

38: PICKLED JALAPEÑO AND CILANTRO HOT SAUCE

Yield: 1.5 cups

Preparation Time: 15 minutes

Scoville: 2,500 - 5,000 SHU

Ingredients

- 1 cup pickled jalapeños, sliced
- 1/2 cup fresh cilantro leaves, packed
- 1/2 medium onion, chopped
- 3 cloves garlic, minced
- 1/4 cup pickle brine
- 1/4 cup apple cider vinegar
- 1 tablespoon lime juice
- 1 tablespoon honey
- 1 teaspoon salt

Instructions

1. *Preparation:*
   - Wear kitchen gloves to handle the pickled jalapeños safely. Slice the pickled jalapeños. Chop the onion and mince the garlic. Pack the fresh cilantro leaves.
2. *Blending:*
   - In a blender, combine the pickled jalapeños, fresh cilantro leaves, chopped onion, minced garlic, pickle brine, apple cider vinegar, lime juice, honey, and salt.
   - Blend until smooth. If the sauce is too thick, add a little water a tablespoon at a time until the desired consistency is reached.
3. *Straining (Optional)*

The sauce can be kept refrigerated for up to a month.

Nutritional Information (per tablespoon): Calories: 10, Total Fat: 0g, Sodium: 130mg, Total Carbohydrates: 2g, Sugars: 1g, Protein: 0g

Tips

- This sauce pairs well with tacos, grilled meats, and as a tangy topping for sandwiches.

39: FERMENTED POMEGRANATE ROSE HOT SAUCE

Yield: 2 cups	Prep Time: 15 minutes	Scoville: 2,500 - 8,000
	Fermentation Time: 2 weeks	SHU

Ingredients

- 6 red jalapeño peppers, stemmed and chopped
- 1/2 cup pomegranate seeds
- 1/2 cup pomegranate juice
- 1/4 cup apple cider vinegar
- 1/4 cup water
- 2 cloves garlic, minced
- 1 tablespoon sea salt
- 1 tablespoon honey
- 1 teaspoon dried rose petals

Instructions

1. *Preparation:*
   - Remove the stems and chop the peppers. Mince the garlic.
2. *Fermentation Setup:*
   - In a sterilized glass jar, combine the chopped red jalapeño peppers, pomegranate seeds, minced garlic, sea salt, and dried rose petals.
   - Mix the pomegranate juice, apple cider vinegar, and water in a separate bowl. Pour this mixture over the ingredients in the jar, ensuring they are fully submerged. If needed, use a fermentation weight to keep them submerged.
   - Cover the jar with a cheesecloth or fermentation lid to allow gases to escape while keeping contaminants out.
3. *Fermentation:*
   - Let the mixture ferment at room temperature for 2 weeks. Check daily to ensure the ingredients remain submerged and to release any built-up gases.
4. *Blending:*
   - After 2 weeks, transfer the fermented mixture to a blender. Add the honey and blend until smooth.

Nutritional Information (per tablespoon): Calories: 10, Total Fat: 0g, Sodium: 120mg, Total Carbohydrates: 2g, Sugars: 1g, Protein: 0g

Tips

- The combination of pomegranate and rose petals adds a unique floral and fruity flavor that pairs well with poultry,and as a glaze for roasted vegetables.

40: CARAMELIZED ONION HOT SAUCE

Yield: 2 cups	Prep Time: 10 minutes	Scoville: 10,000 - 23,000
	Cook Time: 40 minutes	SHU (depending on the serrano peppers)

Ingredients

- 4 large onions, thinly sliced
- 6 red serrano peppers, finely chopped
- 1/2 cup apple cider vinegar
- 1/4 cup olive oil
- 3 cloves garlic, minced
- 1 tablespoon honey
- 1 teaspoon salt
- 1/2 teaspoon black pepper

Instructions

1. *Caramelizing Onions:*
    - Heat olive oil in a large skillet over medium heat.
    - Place the thinly sliced onions to the skillet and sauté, stirring occasionally, until they begin to soften (about 10 minutes).
    - Sprinkle in the brown sugar and continue to cook the onions, stirring frequently, until they turn a deep golden brown and are fully caramelized. This should take about 20 minutes.
2. *Adding Ingredients:*
    - Add chopped serrano peppers and minced garlic to the pan. Cook for 5 minutes, stirring occasionally.
    - Stir in apple cider vinegar, honey, salt, and black pepper. Simmer for 5 minutes.

the sauce can be kept refrigerated for up to a month.

Nutritional Information (per tablespoon): Calories: 15, Total Fat: 1g, Sodium: 85mg, Total Carbohydrates: 3g, Sugars: 2g, Protein: 0g

Tips

- This sauce pairs well with grilled meats, sandwiches, and as a topping for burgers.
- Store in a cool, dark place to maintain flavor and texture.

41: CHIPOTLE-GARLIC HOT SAUCE

Yield: 2 cups   **Prep Time: 15 minutes**   **Scoville: 2,500 - 8,000 SHU**
Cook Time: 30 minutes

Ingredients

- 6 dried chipotle peppers
- 2 fresh jalapeño peppers, stemmed and chopped
- 4 cloves garlic, minced
- 1 medium onion, chopped
- 1 cup distilled white vinegar
- 1 cup water
- 1 teaspoon salt
- 1 teaspoon smoked paprika
- 1 tablespoon brown sugar

Instructions

1. *Preparation:*
   - Remove the stems and chop the peppers.
2. *Cooking:*
   - In a large, heavy-bottomed pot, combine the dried chipotle peppers, fresh jalapeños, garlic, onion, vinegar, and water.
   - Bring the mixture to a boil over medium-high heat. Reduce the heat to low and simmer for about 20-30 minutes, or until the chipotles are soft and the onions are translucent.
3. *Blending:*
   - Remove the pot from the heat and let the mixture cool slightly.
   - Transfer the mixture to a high-speed blender. Add the salt, smoked paprika, and brown sugar.
   - Blend until the sauce is smooth. If the sauce is too thick, add additional water a little at a time until the desired consistency is reached.
4. *Straining:*
   - Pour the blended mixture through a fine-mesh sieve into a bowl to remove any remaining solids, ensuring a smooth texture.

Nutritional Information (per tablespoon): Calories: 10, Total Fat: 0g, Sodium: 120mg, Total Carbohydrates: 2g, Sugars: 1g, Protein: 0g

Tips

- For a smokier flavor, add an extra teaspoon of smoked paprika. This sauce pairs particularly well with roasted vegetables and as a marinade for barbecued dishes.

42: CURRY-INFUSED HABANERO HOT SAUCE

Yield: 2 cups	Prep Time: 15 minutes	Scoville: 100,000 - 350,000
	Cook Time: 15 minutes	SHU
	Fermentation Time: 5 days (optional)	

Ingredients

- 6 habanero peppers, stemmed and chopped
- 1/2 medium onion, chopped
- 3 cloves garlic, minced
- 1 tablespoon curry powder
- 1/2 cup white vinegar
- 1/4 cup lime juice
- 1 tablespoon honey
- 1 teaspoon salt
- 1/4 cup water

Instructions

1. *Preparation:*
   o Remove the stems and chop the peppers. Chop the onion and mince the garlic.
2. *Cooking:*
   o In a medium saucepan, combine the chopped habanero peppers, onion, garlic, curry powder, vinegar, lime juice, honey, salt, and water.
   o Bring the mixture to a boil over medium-high heat. Reduce the heat to low and let it simmer for about 15 minutes, or until the ingredients are soft.
3. *Blending:*
   o Allow the mixture to cool slightly before transferring it to a blender.
   o Blend until smooth. If the sauce is too thick, add more water a tablespoon at a time until the desired consistency is reached.
4. *Straining (Optional)*
5. *Fermentation (Optional)*

The sauce can be kept refrigerated for several months.

Nutritional Information (per tablespoon): Calories: 10, Total Fat: 0g, Sodium: 90mg, Total Carbohydrates: 2g, Sugars: 1g, Protein: 0g

Tips

- This sauce pairs well with grilled meats, rice dishes, and as a marinade for tofu.
- For a thicker consistency, simmer the sauce longer or add a small amount of tomato paste.

43: BLAZING INFERNO MULTI-PEPPER HOT SAUCE

Yield: 1.5 cups	Prep Time: 15 minutes	Scoville: 300,000 -
	Cook Time: 15 minutes	2,200,000 SHU

Ingredients

- 4 Carolina Reaper peppers, stemmed and chopped
- 3 ghost peppers (Bhut Jolokia), stemmed and chopped
- 3 habanero peppers, stemmed and chopped
- 2 scotch bonnet peppers, stemmed and chopped
- 1/2 cup apple cider vinegar
- 1/4 cup lime juice
- 4 cloves garlic, minced
- 1 tablespoon honey
- 1 teaspoon salt
- 1/2 teaspoon smoked paprika

Instructions

1. *Preparation:*
   - Wear kitchen gloves and consider using eye protection when handling the peppers. Remove the stems and chop the Carolina Reaper, ghost, habanero, and scotch bonnet peppers. Mince the garlic.
2. *Cooking:*
   - In a medium saucepan, combine the chopped peppers, garlic, apple cider vinegar, lime juice, honey, salt, and smoked paprika.
   - Bring the mixture to a simmer over medium heat. Reduce the heat to low and let it simmer for about 15 minutes, stirring occasionally, until the peppers are soft and the flavors are well combined.
3. *Blending:*
   - Allow the mixture to cool slightly before transferring it to a blender.
   - Blend until smooth. If the sauce is too thick, add more water a tablespoon at a time until the desired consistency is reached.
4. *Straining (Optional)*

The sauce can be kept refrigerated for several months.

Nutritional Information (per tablespoon): Calories: 12, Total Fat: 0g, Sodium: 90mg, Total Carbohydrates: 2g, Sugars: 1g, Protein: 0g

Tips

- This sauce is not for the faint-hearted; it's designed for true chili heads who crave intense heat. Use it sparingly to add serious fire to your dishes.

44: BOB'S HABANERO HOT SAUCE - LIQUID FIRE

Yield: 2 cups   **Prep Time: 20 minutes**   **Scoville: 100,000 - 350,000**
              Cook time: 15 minutes   **SHU**

Ingredients

- 12 habanero peppers, stemmed and chopped
- 2 medium carrots, peeled and chopped
- 1 medium onion, chopped
- 4 cloves garlic, minced
- 1/2 cup apple cider vinegar
- 1/4 cup lime juice
- 1/4 cup orange juice
- 1 tablespoon honey
- 1 teaspoon salt

Instructions

1. *Preparation:*
   - Remove the stems and chop the peppers. Peel and chop the carrots, chop the onion, and mince the garlic.
2. *Cooking:*
   - In a medium saucepan, combine the chopped habanero peppers, carrots, onion, garlic, apple cider vinegar, lime juice, orange juice, honey, and salt.
   - Bring the mixture to a boil over medium-high heat. Reduce the heat to low and let it simmer for about 15 minutes, or until the carrots are soft.
3. *Blending:*
   - Allow the mixture to cool slightly before transferring it to a blender.
   - Blend until smooth. If the sauce is too thick, add water a tablespoon at a time until the desired consistency is reached.
4. *Straining (Optional)*

The sauce can be kept refrigerated for several months.

Nutritional Information (per tablespoon):   Calories: 10, Total Fat: 0g, Sodium: 85mg, Total Carbohydrates: 2g, Sugars: 1g, Protein: 0g

Tips

- The combination of citrus juices (lime and orange) adds a refreshing, tangy flavor that balances the intense heat of the habaneros.
- This sauce pairs well with grilled meats, seafood, and as a spicy addition to soups and stews.

45: CLASSIC LOUISIANA-STYLE HOT SAUCE

Yield: 2 cups

Prep Time: 10 minutes
Cook Time: 25 minutes
Fermentation Time: 7 days (optional)

Scoville: 30,000 - 50,000 SHU

Ingredients
- 20 fresh cayenne peppers, stemmed
- 4 cloves garlic, minced
- 1 cup distilled white vinegar
- 1/2 cup water
- 1 teaspoon salt
- 1 teaspoon sugar
- 1 tablespoon vegetable oil

Instructions

1. Preparation
- Remove the stems of the peppers and leave the seeds intact for added heat.

2. Cooking
- In a medium saucepan, heat the vegetable oil over medium heat. Add the minced garlic and sauté for 1-2 minutes until fragrant.
- Add the cayenne peppers, vinegar, water, salt, and sugar to the pot. Stir to combine.

3. Simmering
- Bring the mixture to a boil, then reduce the heat to low. Let it simmer for about 20 minutes, or until the peppers are soft and the flavors have melded together.

4. Blending
- Allow the mixture to cool slightly before transferring it to a blender.
- Blend until smooth. If the sauce is too thick, add more water a tablespoon at a time until the desired consistency is reached.

5. Straining
- For a smooth texture, strain the blended sauce through a fine-mesh sieve into a bowl, discarding any solids.

6. Fermentation (Optional)
The sauce can be kept refrigerated for several months.

Nutritional Information (per tablespoon): Calories: 5, Total Fat: 0.2g, Sodium: 120mg, Total Carbohydrates: 1g, Sugars: 0.3g, Protein: 0g

Tips
- For a different flavor, try using apple cider vinegar instead of distilled white vinegar. This sauce is perfect for adding a kick to dishes like gumbo, jambalaya, or just drizzling on eggs.

Yield: 1.5 cups

Prep Time: 10 minutes
Cook time: 15 minutes

Scoville: 2,500 - 8,000 SHU

Ingredients

- 10 fresh jalapeño peppers, stemmed and chopped
- 2 cloves garlic, minced
- 1 small onion, chopped
- 1/2 cup apple cider vinegar
- 1/4 cup water
- 1 tablespoon lime juice
- 1 tablespoon honey
- 1 teaspoon salt
- 1/2 teaspoon cumin

Instructions

1. *Preparation:*
   - Wear kitchen gloves to handle the jalapeño peppers safely. Remove the stems and chop the peppers. Chop the onion and mince the garlic.

2. *Cooking:*
   - In a medium saucepan, combine the chopped jalapeño peppers, onion, garlic, apple cider vinegar, water, lime juice, honey, salt, and cumin.
   - Bring the mixture to a boil over medium-high heat. Reduce the heat to low and let it simmer for about 15 minutes, or until the peppers are soft and the flavors are well combined.

3. *Blending:*
   - Allow the mixture to cool slightly before transferring it to a blender.
   - Blend until smooth. If the sauce is too thick, add more water a tablespoon at a time until the desired consistency is reached.

4. *Straining (Optional)*

The sauce can be kept refrigerated for several weeks.

Nutritional Information (per tablespoon):   Calories: 8, Total Fat: 0g, Sodium: 80mg, Total Carbohydrates: 2g, Sugars: 1g, Protein: 0g

Tips

- This Texas-style hot sauce pairs well with barbecue, tacos, grilled meats, and as a spicy condiment for eggs or sandwiches.

47: BURMAN'S INSPIRED HOT SAUCE

| Yield: 1.5 cups | Prep Time: 10 minutes | Scoville: 30,000 – 50,000 |
| | Cook Time: 15 minutes | SHU |

Ingredients

- 8 cayenne peppers, stemmed and chopped
- 4 Fresno peppers, stemmed and chopped
- 1/2 cup distilled white vinegar
- 1/4 cup water
- 1 tablespoon salt
- 1 tablespoon sugar
- 1/2 teaspoon garlic powder
- 1/2 teaspoon onion powder

Instructions

1. *Preparation:*
   - Remove the stems and chop the peppers.
2. *Cooking:*
   - In a medium saucepan, combine the chopped peppers, white vinegar, water, salt, sugar, garlic powder, and onion powder.
   - Bring the mixture to a boil over medium-high heat. Reduce the heat to low and let it simmer for about 15 minutes, or until the peppers are soft and the flavors are well combined.
3. *Blending:*
   - Allow the mixture to cool slightly before transferring it to a blender.
   - Blend until smooth. If the sauce is too thick, add more water a tablespoon at a time until the desired consistency is reached.
4. *Straining (Optional)*

The sauce can be kept refrigerated for several months.

Nutritional Information (per tablespoon): Calories: 5m, Total Fat: 0g, Sodium: 180mg, Total Carbohydrates: 1g, Sugars: 0.5g, Protein: 0g

Tips

- This hot sauce pairs well with a variety of dishes, including fried chicken, tacos, and as a spicy condiment for sandwiches.
- If you prefer a more tangy sauce, increase the amount of vinegar or add a splash of lemon juice for extra acidity.

48: ALL-AMERICAN BBQ HOT SAUCE

Yield: 1.5 cups	**Prep Time: 10 minutes**	**Scoville: 2,500 - 8,000 SHU**
	Cook time: 20 minutes	

Ingredients

- 6 chipotle peppers in adobo sauce, chopped
- 4 fresh jalapeño peppers, stemmed and chopped
- 1/2 cup ketchup (preferably a smoky BBQ flavor)
- 1/4 cup apple cider vinegar
- 1/4 cup bourbon
- 2 cloves garlic, minced
- 1 tablespoon honey
- 1 teaspoon Worcestershire sauce
- 1/2 teaspoon smoked paprika

Instructions

1. *Preparation:*
   - Remove the stems and chop the chipotle and jalapeño peppers. Mince the garlic.
2. *Cooking:*
   - In a medium saucepan, combine the chopped chipotle peppers, jalapeño peppers, minced garlic, ketchup, apple cider vinegar, bourbon, honey, Worcestershire sauce, and smoked paprika.
   - Bring the mixture to a simmer over medium heat, stirring occasionally to prevent sticking. Cook for about 15-20 minutes, allowing the flavors to meld together and the sauce to thicken slightly.
3. *Blending:*
   - Allow the mixture to cool slightly before transferring it to a blender.
   - Blend until smooth. If the sauce is too thick, add a little water a tablespoon at a time until the desired consistency is reached.
4. *Straining (Optional)*

The sauce can be kept refrigerated for several weeks.

Nutritional Information (per tablespoon): Calories: 15, Total Fat: 0g, Sodium: 130mg, Total Carbohydrates: 3g, Sugars: 2g, Protein: 0g

Tips

- This All-American BBQ Hot Sauce pairs well with grilled meats, burgers, chicken wings, and as a dip for fries.
- The bourbon adds a warm, rich undertone that complements the smoky chipotle peppers, making this sauce perfect for barbecue lovers.

49: SMOKY BACON JALAPEÑO HOT SAUCE

Yield: 1.5 cups   **Prep Time: 15 minutes**   **Scoville: 2,500 - 8,000 SHU**
Cook time: 25 minutes

Ingredients

- 8 jalapeño peppers, stemmed and chopped
- 4 strips of smoked bacon
- 1/2 cup apple cider vinegar
- 1/4 cup water
- 1 small onion, chopped
- 3 cloves garlic, minced
- 1 tablespoon honey
- 1 teaspoon smoked paprika
- 1/2 teaspoon salt

Instructions

1. *Cooking the Bacon:*
   - In a large skillet, cook the bacon strips over medium heat until they are crispy, about 8-10 minutes.
   - Remove the bacon from the skillet and place it on paper towels to drain excess grease. Once cooled, chop the bacon into small pieces.
   - Reserve about 1 tablespoon of the bacon fat in the skillet for sautéing the vegetables.
2. *Sautéing the Vegetables:*
   - In the same skillet with the reserved bacon fat, add the chopped onion and garlic. Sauté over medium heat until the onion becomes translucent and the garlic is fragrant, about 5 minutes.
   - Add the chopped jalapeño peppers to the skillet and cook for another 3-5 minutes until the peppers are softened.
3. *Cooking the Sauce:*
   - Add the apple cider vinegar, water, honey, smoked paprika, and salt to the skillet. Stir to combine all the ingredients.
   - Bring the mixture to a simmer and let it cook for about 10 minutes, allowing the flavors to meld together.
4. *Blending:*
   - Remove the skillet from heat and allow the mixture to cool slightly. Transfer the cooked mixture to a blender.
   - Add the chopped bacon to the blender and blend until smooth. If the sauce is too thick, add more water a tablespoon at a time until you reach the desired consistency.

5. *Straining (Optional)*

The sauce can be kept refrigerated for several weeks.

Nutritional Information (per tablespoon):   Calories: 20, Total Fat: 1.5g, Sodium: 90mg, Total Carbohydrates: 1g, Sugars: 0.5g, Protein: 1g

Tips

- This smoky bacon jalapeño hot sauce pairs well with burgers, grilled meats, and as a spicy condiment for eggs or sandwiches.
- If you prefer a more pronounced smoky flavor, consider adding an additional teaspoon of smoked paprika or using a more heavily smoked bacon.

50: EGG-INFUSED HOT SAUCE

Yield: 1.5 cups	Prep Time: 15 minutes	Scoville: 30,000 – 50,000
	Cook time: 10 minutes	SHU

Ingredients

- 6 fresh cayenne peppers, stemmed and chopped
- 2 large egg yolks
- 1/2 cup white vinegar
- 1/4 cup water
- 3 cloves garlic, minced
- 1 tablespoon Dijon mustard
- 1 teaspoon honey
- 1 teaspoon salt
- 1/2 teaspoon black pepper

Instructions

1. *Preparation:*
   - Remove the stems and chop the peppers. Mince the garlic. Separate the egg yolks from the whites, reserving the yolks for the sauce.
2. *Cooking:*
   - In a medium saucepan, combine the chopped cayenne peppers, minced garlic, white vinegar, water, Dijon mustard, honey, salt, and black pepper.
   - Bring the mixture to a simmer over medium heat, stirring occasionally. Cook for about 10 minutes until the peppers soften and the flavors meld.
3. *Tempering the Egg Yolks:*
   - In a small bowl, whisk the egg yolks until smooth. To prevent the yolks from curdling, slowly add a small amount of the hot pepper mixture to the yolks while whisking continuously.
   - Once tempered, slowly whisk the yolk mixture back into the saucepan with the hot sauce.
4. *Blending:*
   - Remove the saucepan from heat and allow the mixture to cool slightly. Transfer the sauce to a blender and blend until smooth.
   - If the sauce is too thick, add more water a tablespoon at a time until the desired consistency is reached.

The sauce can be kept refrigerated for up to two weeks.

Nutritional Information (per tablespoon): Calories: 15, Total Fat: 1g, Sodium: 120mg, Total Carbohydrates: 1g, Sugars: 0.5g. Protein: 1g

Tips

- This egg-infused hot sauce pairs well with breakfast dishes like scrambled eggs, omelets, and breakfast sandwiches, adding a rich, creamy heat.
- Be careful when tempering the egg yolks to avoid scrambling them; whisking constantly while adding the hot mixture ensures a smooth sauce.

51: NEW YORK-STYLE DELI HOT SAUCE

Yield: 1.5 cups	Prep Time: 15 minutes	Scoville: 10,000 - 23,000
	Cook time: 10 minutes	SHU

Ingredients

- 6 red serrano peppers, stemmed and chopped
- 1/2 cup dill pickle brine
- 1/4 cup yellow mustard
- 2 tablespoons prepared horseradish
- 1 small onion, chopped
- 3 cloves garlic, minced
- 1 tablespoon apple cider vinegar
- 1 tablespoon honey
- 1/2 teaspoon celery seed

Instructions

1. *Preparation:*
   - Remove the stems and chop the peppers. Mince the garlic and chop the onion.
2. *Cooking:*
   - In a medium saucepan, combine the chopped serrano peppers, dill pickle brine, yellow mustard, prepared horseradish, chopped onion, minced garlic, apple cider vinegar, honey, and celery seed.
   - Bring the mixture to a simmer over medium heat, stirring occasionally. Cook for about 10 minutes, allowing the flavors to meld together.
3. *Blending:*
   - Allow the mixture to cool slightly before transferring it to a blender.
   - Blend until smooth. If the sauce is too thick, add a little more pickle brine or water, a tablespoon at a time, until the desired consistency is reached.
4. *Straining (Optional)*
5. *Bottling:*
   - Transfer the hot sauce to sterilized bottles using a funnel. Seal tightly and store in the refrigerator. The sauce can be kept refrigerated for several weeks.

Nutritional Information (per tablespoon): Calories: 10, Total Fat: 0g, Sodium: 120mg, Total Carbohydrates: 2g, Sugars: 1g, Protein: 0g

Tips

- This New York-Style Deli Hot Sauce is perfect for adding a spicy kick to pastrami sandwiches, hot dogs, bagels with lox, and as a unique condiment for pretzels.
- The dill pickle brine and mustard give this sauce a tangy, savory flavor that's reminiscent of classic New York deli flavors.

52: AJI CHOMBO HOT SAUCE

Yield: 2 cups

Prep Time: 15 minutes
Cook time: 15 minutes

Scoville: 100,000 - 350,000
SHU

Ingredients

- 10 habanero peppers, stemmed and chopped
- 1 medium carrot, peeled and chopped
- 1 medium onion, chopped
- 4 cloves garlic, minced
- 1/2 cup white vinegar
- 1/4 cup lime juice
- 1/4 cup water
- 1 tablespoon mustard
- 1 teaspoon salt

Instructions

1. *Preparation:*
   - Remove the stems and chop the peppers. Peel and chop the carrot, chop the onion, and mince the garlic.
2. *Cooking:*
   - In a medium saucepan, combine the chopped habanero peppers, carrot, onion, garlic, white vinegar, lime juice, water, mustard, and salt.
   - Bring the mixture to a boil over medium-high heat. Reduce the heat to low and let it simmer for about 15 minutes, or until the carrots are soft and the flavors are well combined.
3. *Blending:*
   - Allow the mixture to cool.
   - Blend until smooth. If the sauce is too thick, add more water a tablespoon at a time until the desired consistency is reached.
4. *Straining (Optional)*

The sauce can be kept refrigerated for several months.

Nutritional Information (per tablespoon): Calories: 8, Total Fat: 0g, Sodium: 85mg, Total Carbohydrates: 2g, Sugars: 0.5g, Protein: 0g

Tips

- Aji Chombo is a traditional Panamanian hot sauce that pairs well with grilled meats, seafood, and as a spicy condiment for rice and beans.

53: CHERMOULA HOT SAUCE

Yield: 1.5 cups	Prep Time: 15 minutes Fermentation Time: 3 days (optional)	Scoville: 5,000 - 10,000 SHU

Ingredients

- 1 cup fresh cilantro, chopped
- 1 cup fresh parsley, chopped
- 3 cloves garlic, minced
- 2 red chili peppers, stemmed and chopped
- 1 teaspoon ground cumin
- 1 teaspoon ground coriander
- 1/2 teaspoon smoked paprika
- 1/2 cup olive oil
- 1/4 cup lemon juice
- 1 teaspoon salt

Instructions

1. *Preparation:*
   - Remove the stems and chop the peppers. Chop the fresh cilantro and parsley, and mince the garlic.
2. *Mixing:*
   - In a large mixing bowl, combine the chopped cilantro, parsley, minced garlic, chopped red chili peppers, ground cumin, ground coriander, and smoked paprika.
   - Stir in the olive oil, lemon juice, and salt. Mix thoroughly to ensure all ingredients are well combined.
3. *Blending:*
   - Transfer the mixture to a blender and blend until smooth. If the sauce is too thick, add a little water a tablespoon at a time until the desired consistency is reached.
4. *Fermentation (Optional):*

The sauce can be kept refrigerated for up to a month.

Nutritional Information (per tablespoon): Calories: 45, Total Fat: 5g, Sodium: 85mg, Total Carbohydrates: 1g, Sugars: 0g, Protein: 0g

Tips

- Chermoula is a traditional North African sauce, and this hot version pairs well with grilled fish, meats, and vegetables.
- The combination of fresh herbs and spices gives the sauce a vibrant and aromatic flavor. Adjust the spices to your taste preference.

54: GOCHUJANG SAUCE

Yield: 2 cups

Prep Time: 15 minutes

Cook Time: 10 minutes

Fermentation Time:

1 month

Scoville: 1,000 - 5,000 SHU

Ingredients

- 1 cup gochugaru (Korean red chili powder)
- 1/2 cup sweet rice flour (mochiko)
- 1/2 cup water
- 1/4 cup soy sauce
- 1/4 cup rice vinegar
- 1/4 cup honey
- 2 tablespoons miso paste
- 4 cloves garlic, minced
- 1 tablespoon salt

Instructions

1. *Making Rice Paste:*
   - In a small saucepan, combine the sweet rice flour and water. Cook over medium heat, stirring constantly, until it forms a thick paste (about 5-7 minutes). Remove from heat and let it cool.

2. *Mixing Ingredients:*
   - In a large mixing bowl, combine the gochugaru, soy sauce, rice vinegar, honey, miso paste, minced garlic, and salt.
   - Add the cooled rice paste to the mixture and stir until well combined. The mixture should be smooth and thick.

3. *Fermentation Setup:*
   - Transfer the mixture to a sterilized glass jar, pressing down to remove any air pockets.
   - Cover the jar with a cheesecloth or fermentation lid to allow gases to escape while keeping contaminants out.

4. *Fermentation:*
   - Let the mixture ferment at room temperature for about 1 month. Stir the mixture once a week and check for any mold or off smells. The sauce should develop a rich flavor.

The sauce can be kept refrigerated for several months.

Nutritional Information (per tablespoon): Calories: 25, Total Fat: 0g,Sodium: 300mg, Total Carbohydrates: 6g, Sugars: 3g, Protein: 1g

Tips

- Gochujang is a staple in Korean cuisine and pairs well with meats, vegetables, and as a base for marinades and sauces.

55: SPICY BASIL PESTO SAUCE

Yield: 1 cup   **Prep Time: 15 minutes**   **Scoville: 10,000 - 23,000 SHU**

Ingredients

- 2 cups fresh basil leaves
- 3 serrano peppers, stemmed and chopped
- 1/2 cup grated Parmesan cheese
- 1/2 cup pine nuts, toasted
- 3 cloves garlic, minced
- 1/2 cup extra virgin olive oil
- 1 tablespoon lemon juice
- 1 teaspoon salt
- 1/2 teaspoon black pepper

Instructions

1. *Preparation:*
   - Remove the stems and chop the peppers. Toast the pine nuts in a dry skillet over medium heat until golden brown, then let them cool.
2. *Blending:*
   - In a food processor or blender, combine the basil leaves, serrano peppers, Parmesan cheese, toasted pine nuts, and minced garlic.
   - Pulse until the ingredients are coarsely chopped.
3. *Adding Olive Oil:*
   - While the food processor is running, slowly add the extra virgin olive oil in a steady stream. Blend until the mixture is smooth and well combined.
4. *Seasoning:*
   - Add the lemon juice, salt, and black pepper to the pesto. Pulse a few more times to incorporate all the ingredients.

The sauce can be kept refrigerated for up to a week.

Nutritional Information (per tablespoon): Calories: 90, Total Fat: 9g, Sodium: 120mg, Total Carbohydrates: 1g, Sugars: 0g, Protein: 2g

Tips

- This pairs well with pasta, grilled chicken, and as a spread for sandwiches.
- To preserve the vibrant green color, blanch the basil leaves in boiling water for 5-10 seconds, then immediately plunge them into ice water before blending.
- Pine nuts can be expensive; feel free to substitute with walnuts or almonds if desired.

56: ZHUG (YEMENITE HOT SAUCE)

Yield: 1 cup   **Prep Time: 15 minutes**   **Scoville: 10,000 - 23,000 SHU**

Ingredients

- 1 cup fresh cilantro leaves, packed
- 1 cup fresh parsley leaves, packed
- 4 green chilies stemmed & chopped
- 4 cloves garlic, minced
- 1 teaspoon ground cumin
- 1 teaspoon ground coriander
- 1/2 teaspoon ground cardamom
- 1/2 teaspoon salt
- 1/4 cup olive oil
- 2 tablespoons lemon juice

Instructions

1. *Preparation:*
   - Remove the stems and chop the chilies. Mince the garlic.
2. *Blending:*
   - In a food processor or blender, combine the cilantro, parsley, chopped chilies, minced garlic, cumin, coriander, cardamom, and salt.
   - Blend until the ingredients are finely chopped.
3. *Adding Olive Oil and Lemon Juice:*
   - While the food processor is running, gradually pour the olive oil and lemon juice. Blend until the mixture is smooth and well combined.
4. *Storing:*
   - Transfer the zhug to a sterilized jar or airtight container. Seal tightly and store in the refrigerator. The sauce can be kept refrigerated for up to a week.

Nutritional Information (per tablespoon): Calories: 45, Total Fat: 4.5g, Sodium: 75mg, Total Carbohydrates: 1g, Sugars: 0g, Protein: 0g

Tips

- Zhug pairs well with grilled meats, falafel, shawarma, and as a spicy condiment for sandwiches and wraps.
- Freshly ground spices can enhance the flavor of the zhug, so consider toasting and grinding whole spices if possible.

57: PERI PERI SAUCE

Yield: 1 cup	Prep Time: 15 minutes	Scoville: 100,000 - 225,000
	Cook Time: 10 minutes	SHU

Ingredients

- 10 red bird's eye chilies, stemmed and chopped
- 4 cloves garlic, minced
- 1/4 cup olive oil
- 1/4 cup white vinegar
- 1 small red bell pepper, chopped
- 1 teaspoon smoked paprika
- 1 teaspoon dried oregano
- 1 teaspoon salt
- 1 tablespoon lemon juice

Instructions

1. *Preparation:*
   - Remove the stems and chop the chilies. Mince the garlic and chop the red bell pepper.
2. *Cooking:*
   - In a medium saucepan, combine the chopped bird's eye chilies, garlic, olive oil, white vinegar, red bell pepper, smoked paprika, dried oregano, and salt.
   - Bring the mixture to a simmer over medium heat. Reduce the heat to low and let it simmer for about 10 minutes, stirring occasionally to prevent burning.
3. *Blending:*
   - Allow the mixture to cool slightly before transferring it to a blender.
   - Add the lemon juice and blend until smooth. If the sauce is too thick, add a little water a tablespoon at a time until the desired consistency is reached.
4. *Straining*

The sauce can be kept refrigerated for several months.

Nutritional Information (per tablespoon): Calories: 35, Total Fat: 3.5g, Sodium: 120mg, Total Carbohydrates: 1g, Sugars: 0g, Protein: 0g

Tips

- Peri peri sauce pairs well with grilled chicken, seafood, as a marinade for meats and vegetables, as a dipping sauce for fries and roasted vegetables for a spicy kick.

58: JAPANESE YUZU KOSHO

Yield: 1/2 cup	Prep Time: 15 minutes Fermentation Time: 1 week	Scoville: 50,000 - 100,000 SHU

Ingredients

- 4 yuzu fruits (zest only)
- 6 green Thai bird's eye chilies, stemmed and chopped
- 1 tablespoon sea salt
- 1 tablespoon fresh yuzu juice (or substitute with lemon juice if yuzu is unavailable)
- 1 tablespoon sake (optional)

Instructions

1. *Preparation:*
   - Remove the stems from the Thai bird's eye chilies and chop them. Carefully zest the yuzu fruits, ensuring to avoid the bitter white pith.
2. *Blending:*
   - In a mortar and pestle (or a food processor), combine the yuzu zest, chopped chilies, sea salt, and fresh yuzu juice.
   - Grind the ingredients together until they form a coarse paste. If you prefer a smoother consistency, continue grinding until desired texture is achieved.
3. *Optional Addition:*
   - Add the sake to the mixture for a slightly milder flavor and enhanced preservation. Mix well.
4. *Fermentation:*
   - Transfer the paste to a sterilized glass jar. Seal the jar and allow the yuzu kosho to ferment at room temperature for 1 week. This fermentation process enhances the flavors and adds complexity.

It can be kept refrigerated for up to 3 months.

Nutritional Information (per teaspoon): Calories: 2, Total Fat: 0g, Sodium: 100mg, Total Carbohydrates: 0g, Sugars: 0g, Protein: 0g

Tips

- If yuzu is unavailable, you can substitute the zest and juice with a combination of lemon, lime, and grapefruit to mimic the unique citrus flavor of yuzu.
- Yuzu kosho is traditionally used as a condiment for grilled meats, sushi, sashimi, and hot pot dishes. A little goes a long way, as the flavor is intensely aromatic and spicy.

59: SPICY INDIAN MASALA HOT SAUCE

Yield: 1.5 cups   **Prep Time: 15 minutes**   Scoville: 30,000 - 50,000
                        Cook Time: 20 minutes   SHU (depending on the
                                                      combination of chilies)

Ingredients

- 6 dried Kashmiri red chilies, stemmed and soaked in warm water
- 2 fresh green chilies (like serrano or Thai), chopped
- 1/2 cup white vinegar
- 1/4 cup tomato paste
- 1 small onion, chopped
- 4 cloves garlic, minced
- 1 tablespoon ginger, minced
- 1 teaspoon cumin seeds
- 1 teaspoon garam masala
- 1 teaspoon salt

Instructions

1. *Preparation:*
   - Soak the dried Kashmiri red chilies in warm water for about 10 minutes until softened. Chop the fresh green chilies, onion, garlic, and ginger.
2. *Cooking:*
   - Heat a medium saucepan over medium heat. Add the cumin seeds and toast for about 1 minute until fragrant.
   - Add the chopped onion, garlic, and ginger to the pan and sauté until the onion becomes translucent.
3. *Blending:*
   - Transfer the sautéed mixture to a blender. Add the soaked red chilies, chopped green chilies, tomato paste, vinegar, garam masala, and salt. Blend until smooth.
   - If the sauce is too thick, add a little water a tablespoon at a time until the desired consistency is reached.
4. *Cooking Again:*
   - Return the blended mixture to the saucepan and simmer over low heat for about 10 minutes, stirring occasionally to allow the flavors to meld together.

The sauce can be kept refrigerated for several weeks.

Nutritional Information (per tablespoon): Calories: 10, Total Fat: 0g, Sodium: 75mg, Total Carbohydrates: 2g, Sugars: 0.5g, Protein: 0g

- This Indian-inspired hot sauce pairs well with grilled meats, curries, rice dishes, and as a spicy condiment for snacks like samosas or pakoras.
- The Kashmiri red chilies provide a vibrant red color and a mild heat, while the garam masala adds a warm, complex spice profile.

60: SAMBAL OELEK

Yield: 1 cup	Prep Time: 10 minutes	Scoville: 30,000 - 50,000
	Fermentation time:	SHU
	Optional, 3 days	

Ingredients

- 10 fresh red chilies (such as red Fresno or Thai chilies), stemmed and chopped
- 2 cloves garlic, minced
- 2 tablespoons white vinegar
- 1 tablespoon lime juice
- 1 teaspoon salt
- 1 teaspoon sugar

Instructions

1. *Preparation:*
   - Remove the stems from the chilies and chop them. Mince the garlic.
2. *Blending:*
   - In a mortar and pestle (or food processor), combine the chopped chilies, minced garlic, vinegar, lime juice, salt, and sugar.
   - Grind the ingredients together until they form a coarse paste. Sambal Oelek should have a slightly chunky texture, so avoid over-blending.
3. Fermentation (Optional):
   - For deeper flavors, transfer the mixture to a sterilized glass jar. Cover it loosely with a lid or cheesecloth and let it ferment at room temperature for about 3 days. Stir the mixture daily and ensure it remains submerged.

The sauce can be kept refrigerated for up to a month.

Nutritional Information (per tablespoon): Calories: 5, Total Fat: 0g, Sodium: 90mg, Total Carbohydrates: 1g, Sugars: 0.5g, Protein: 0g

Tips

- Sambal Oelek is a versatile condiment used in Indonesian and Malaysian cuisine, perfect for adding heat to stir-fries, noodles, and marinades.
- Ensure to use fresh chilies for the best flavor. If using dried chilies, rehydrate them in warm water before blending.

61: MALAGUETA PEPPER SAUCE (BRAZIL)

Yield: 1.5 cups	Prep Time: 10 minutes	Scoville: 60,000 - 100,000
	Cook time: 10 minutes	SHU
	Fermentation time:	
	Optional, 1 week	

Ingredients

- 15 fresh malagueta peppers, stemmed and chopped
- 4 cloves garlic, minced
- 1/2 cup white vinegar
- 1/4 cup olive oil
- 1 teaspoon salt
- 1 teaspoon sugar
- 1/2 teaspoon dried oregano

Instructions

1. *Preparation:*
   - Remove the stems and chop the peppers. Mince the garlic.
2. *Sautéing:*
   - In a medium saucepan, heat the olive oil over medium heat. Add the minced garlic and sauté for about 2 minutes until fragrant, but not browned.
   - Add the chopped malagueta peppers to the saucepan and cook for another 3-4 minutes, stirring occasionally.
3. *Simmering:*
   - Add the white vinegar, salt, sugar, and dried oregano to the saucepan. Stir to combine.
   - Bring the mixture to a simmer and let it cook for about 5 minutes, allowing the flavors to meld together.
4. *Blending:*
   - Remove the saucepan from heat and let the mixture cool slightly. Transfer the mixture to a blender and blend until smooth.
   - If the sauce is too thick, add a little more vinegar or water, a tablespoon at a time, until the desired consistency is reached.
5. *Fermentation (Optional)*

The sauce can be kept refrigerated for up to two months.

Nutritional Information (per tablespoon): Calories: 15, Total Fat: 1g, Sodium: 85mg, Total Carbohydrates: 1g, Sugars: 0.5g, Protein: 0g

Tips

- This Malagueta Pepper Sauce is a staple in Brazilian cuisine, often served with grilled meats, feijoada, and as a condiment for various dishes

62: PERI-PERI SHRIMP SKEWERS

Yield: 4 servings | **Prep Time: 15 minutes** | **Cook Time: 8-10 minutes**
(8 skewers) | **Marination Time:**
| **30 minutes**

Ingredients

- 1 lb large shrimp, peeled and deveined
- 1/2 cup Peri-Peiri sauce (see recipe 57)
- 2 tablespoons olive oil
- 1 tablespoon lemon juice
- 2 cloves garlic, minced
- 1 teaspoon smoked paprika
- 1/2 teaspoon salt
- Fresh lemon wedges, for serving

Instructions

1. *Preparation:*
   - In a large mixing bowl, combine the Peri-Peri sauce, olive oil, lemon juice, minced garlic, smoked paprika, and salt.
   - Add the shrimp to the bowl, tossing to coat them evenly with the marinade.
2. *Marinating:*
   - Seal the bowl with plastic wrap and chill for at least 30 minutes to let the shrimp soak up the flavors of the Peri-Peri sauce.
3. *Skewering:*
   - Preheat your grill to medium-high heat.
   - Thread the marinated shrimp onto skewers, about 4-5 shrimp per skewer. If using wooden skewers, soak them in water for 15-20 minutes before grilling to prevent them from burning.
4. *Grilling:*
   - Place the skewers on the preheated grill. Cook for 3-4 minutes on each side, or until the shrimp are opaque, pink, and have a slight char. Be careful not to overcook them, as shrimp can become tough.
5. *Serving:*
   - Remove the skewers from the grill and transfer them to a serving platter. Serve with fresh lemon wedges for squeezing over the shrimp.

Nutritional Information (per serving): Calories: 190, Total Fat: 10g, Sodium: 650mg, Total Carbohydrates: 2g, Sugars: 0g, Protein: 22g

Tips

- For an extra burst of flavor, reserve a bit of the Peri-Peri marinade (before adding the shrimp) to brush on the skewers during grilling.
- These Peri-Peri shrimp skewers pair well with grilled vegetables, rice, or a fresh salad.

63: AVOCADO SALAD WITH AVOCADO JALAPENO HOT SAUCE DRESSING

Yield: 4 servings   **Prep Time: 15 minutes**

Ingredients

- 2 ripe avocados, diced
- 1 cucumber, sliced
- 1 cup cherry tomatoes, halved
- 1/4 red onion, thinly sliced
- 1/4 cup fresh cilantro leaves, chopped
- 1/4 cup crumbled feta cheese (optional)
- 2 tablespoons Avocado Jalapeno Hot Sauce
- 1 tablespoon lime juice
- 1 tablespoon olive oil
- Salt and pepper to taste

Instructions

1. *Preparing the Salad:*
   - In a large mixing bowl, combine the diced avocados, sliced cucumber, halved cherry tomatoes, and thinly sliced red onion.
   - Add the chopped cilantro leaves and crumbled feta cheese (if using) to the bowl.
2. *Making the Dressing:*
   - In a small bowl, whisk together the Avocado Jalapeno Hot Sauce, lime juice, and olive oil until well combined.
3. *Tossing the Salad:*
   - Pour the dressing over the salad and gently toss to coat all the ingredients evenly. Season with salt and pepper to taste.
4. *Serving:*
   - Transfer the salad to a serving dish and enjoy immediately as a refreshing side dish or light meal.

Nutritional Information (per serving of salad): Calories: 210, Total Fat: 18g, Sodium: 220mg, Total Carbohydrates: 12g, Sugars: 3g, Protein: 3g

Tips

- For added crunch, top the salad with toasted nuts or seeds.

64: EGG SANDWICH WITH AMERICAN HOT SAUCE

Yield: 1 sandwich

Prep Time: 5 minutes
Cook Time: 5 minutes

Assembly Time: 2 minutes

Ingredients

- 2 large eggs
- 2 slices of bread (your choice)
- 1 tablespoon butter
- 1 slice cheddar cheese (optional)
- 1 tablespoon egg-infused hot sauce (see recipe 51)
- 1 tablespoon mayonnaise
- Salt and pepper to taste
- Optional: Lettuce, tomato, or bacon for extra toppings

Instructions

1. *Preparing the Eggs:*
   - Heat a non-stick skillet over medium heat and add the butter.
   - Crack the eggs into the skillet and cook to your desired doneness (sunny side up, over easy, or scrambled).
   - Season the eggs with salt and pepper to taste.

2. *Toasting the Bread:*
   - While the eggs are cooking, lightly toast the bread slices in a toaster or on a skillet until golden brown.

3. *Assembling the Sandwich:*
   - Spread the mayonnaise on one side of each toasted bread slice.
   - Place the cooked eggs on one slice of the bread. If using, add a slice of cheddar cheese on top of the eggs.
   - Drizzle the American-inspired hot sauce over the eggs and cheese.
   - Add any additional toppings like lettuce, tomato, or bacon if desired.
   - Top with the other slice of bread, mayonnaise side down.

4. *Serving:*
   - Cut the sandwich in half and serve immediately. Enjoy the creamy, spicy flavor of the hot sauce combined with the richness of the eggs and cheese.

Nutritional Information (per sandwich): Calories: 350, Total Fat: 23g, Sodium: 750mg, Total Carbohydrates: 25g, Sugars: 5g, Protein: 12g

Tips

- Customize your sandwich by adding extra toppings like avocado, spinach, or a fried green tomato.

65: GRILLED YUZU KOSHO CHICKEN THIGHS

Yield: 4 servings   **Prep Time: 10 minutes**   **Cook Time: 15 minutes**
Marination Time:
30 minutes

Ingredients
- 4 boneless, skinless chicken thighs
- 2 tablespoons Yuzu Kosho (see recipe 59)
- 2 tablespoons soy sauce
- 1 tablespoon rice vinegar
- 1 tablespoon sesame oil
- 2 teaspoons honey
- 1 clove garlic, minced
- 1 tablespoon fresh lime juice
- 1 teaspoon toasted sesame seeds (optional, for garnish)
- 2 green onions, chopped (optional, for garnish)

Instructions
1. *Marinating the Chicken:*
   - In a large bowl, whisk together the Yuzu Kosho, soy sauce, rice vinegar, sesame oil, honey, minced garlic, and lime juice.
   - Add the chicken thighs to the bowl, turning them to coat evenly with the marinade.
   - Cover the bowl with plastic wrap and refrigerate for at least 30 minutes, allowing the flavors to infuse into the chicken.
2. *Grilling the Chicken:*
   - Preheat your grill to medium-high heat.
   - Remove the chicken from the marinade and let any excess marinade drip off.
   - Place the chicken thighs on the grill and cook for about 6-7 minutes on each side, or until the chicken is cooked through and has a nice char. The internal temperature should reach 165°F (74°C).
3. *Serving:*
   - Transfer the grilled chicken thighs to a serving platter.
   - Garnish with toasted sesame seeds and chopped green onions if desired.
   - Serve hot, accompanied by steamed rice, grilled vegetables, or a fresh salad.

Nutritional Information (per serving): Calories: 220, Total Fat: 12g, Sodium: 600mg, Total Carbohydrates: 6g, Sugars: 3g, Protein: 22g

Tips

- If you don't have a grill, you can also cook the chicken thighs in a hot skillet or under the broiler.
- Adjust the amount of Yuzu Kosho according to your heat preference; it can be quite potent, so a little goes a long way.

66: MANGO HABANERO GLAZED TOFU STIR-FRY

Yield: 4 servings   **Prep Time: 15 minutes**
                               Cook Time: 15 minutes

Ingredients

- 1 block (14 oz) firm tofu, drained and cubed
- 1/4 cup Mango Habanero Hot Sauce (see recipe 14)
- 2 tablespoons soy sauce
- 1 tablespoon honey or maple syrup
- 1 tablespoon lime juice
- 1 tablespoon sesame oil
- 2 cloves garlic, minced
- 1 red bell pepper, sliced
- 1 cup broccoli florets
- 1/2 cup snap peas
- 2 green onions, chopped (optional, for garnish)
- Cooked rice or noodles (for serving)

Instructions

1. *Preparing the Tofu:*
   - Press the tofu to remove excess moisture. Cut the tofu into 1-inch cubes.
   - In a bowl, whisk together the Mango Habanero Hot Sauce, soy sauce, honey or maple syrup, and lime juice. Set aside.

2. *Cooking the Tofu:*
   - Heat sesame oil in a large non-stick skillet or wok over medium-high heat.
   - Add the cubed tofu to the skillet and cook, until golden and crispy on all sides, about 5-7 minutes.
   - Remove the tofu from the skillet and set aside.

3. *Stir-Frying the Vegetables:*
   - In the same skillet, add a little more oil if needed. Add the minced garlic and sauté for about 30 seconds until fragrant.
   - Add the red bell pepper, broccoli, and snap peas. Stir-fry the vegetables for about 3-4 minutes until they are crisp-tender.

4. *Combining the Tofu and Sauce:*
   - Return the cooked tofu to the skillet with the vegetables.
   - Pour the Mango Habanero sauce mixture over the tofu and vegetables. Toss everything together until the tofu and vegetables are evenly coated with the sauce.
   - Cook for another 2-3 minutes, allowing the sauce to thicken slightly and glaze the tofu.

5. *Serving:*
   - Serve the Mango Habanero Glazed Tofu Stir-Fry over cooked rice or noodles.
   - Garnish with chopped green onions, if desired.

Nutritional Information (per serving): Calories: 250, Total Fat: 12g, Sodium: 550mg, Total Carbohydrates: 18g, Sugars: 10g, Protein: 15g

Tips
- For added crunch, sprinkle some toasted sesame seeds or chopped peanuts over the finished dish.

67: CINNAMON HABANERO GLAZED ROASTED SWEET POTATOES

Yield: 4 servings   **Prep Time: 10 minutes**

Cook Time:

30-35 minutes

Ingredients

- 4 medium sweet potatoes, peeled and cut into 1-inch cubes
- 2 tablespoons olive oil
- 1/4 cup Cinnamon Habanero Hot Sauce (see recipe 21)
- 2 tablespoons maple syrup
- 1 teaspoon ground cinnamon
- 1/2 teaspoon salt
- 1/4 teaspoon black pepper
- Fresh cilantro or parsley, chopped (optional, for garnish)

Instructions

1. *Preheating the Oven:*
   - Preheat your oven to 400°F (200°C). Line a baking sheet with parchment paper or lightly grease it with cooking spray.
2. *Preparing the Sweet Potatoes:*
   - In a large mixing bowl, toss the sweet potato cubes with olive oil, salt, and black pepper until evenly coated.
   - Spread the sweet potatoes in a single layer on the prepared baking sheet.
3. *Roasting:*
   - Roast the sweet potatoes in the preheated oven for 20-25 minutes, turning them halfway through, until they are tender and starting to caramelize.
4. *Making the Glaze:*
   - While the sweet potatoes are roasting, prepare the glaze by mixing the Cinnamon Habanero Hot Sauce, maple syrup, and ground cinnamon in a small bowl.
5. *Glazing the Sweet Potatoes:*
   - After 20-25 minutes of roasting, remove the sweet potatoes from the oven. Drizzle the hot sauce glaze over the sweet potatoes, tossing them gently to coat.
   - Return the sweet potatoes to the oven and roast for an additional 5-10 minutes, or until the glaze is bubbling and the sweet potatoes are fully cooked and caramelized.
6. *Serving:*
   - Remove the sweet potatoes from the oven and transfer them to a serving dish. Garnish with chopped cilantro or parsley if desired.
   - Serve hot as a flavorful side dish or a vegetarian main course.

Nutritional Information (per serving): Calories: 220, Total Fat: 7g, Sodium: 300mg, Total Carbohydrates: 38g, Sugars: 16g, Protein: 2g

Tips

- This dish pairs well with roasted meats, grilled chicken, or as part of a holiday meal.
- For a bit of crunch, consider adding toasted pecans or walnuts during the final 5 minutes of roasting.

68: SPICY BLACK BEAN CHILI

Yield: 4-6 servings
Prep Time: 15 minutes
Cook Time: 45 minutes

Ingredients

- 2 tablespoons olive oil
- 1 large onion, chopped
- 4 cloves garlic, minced
- 2 jalapeño peppers, seeded and chopped
- 2 cans (15 oz each) black beans, drained and rinsed
- 1 can (15 oz) diced tomatoes
- 1 can (15 oz) tomato sauce
- 1 cup vegetable or chicken broth
- 1 tablespoon chili powder
- 1 teaspoon cumin
- 1 teaspoon smoked paprika
- 1/2 teaspoon cayenne pepper (adjust to taste)
- 1 teaspoon salt
- 1/2 teaspoon black pepper
- 1/4 cup fresh cilantro, chopped (optional, for garnish)
- Sour cream, shredded cheese, and lime wedges (optional, for serving)

Instructions

1. *Sautéing the Aromatics:*
   - Heat the olive oil in a large pot or Dutch oven over medium heat.
   - Add the chopped onion and sauté for about 5 minutes until it becomes soft and translucent.
   - Add the minced garlic and chopped jalapeño peppers to the pot, and sauté for another 2 minutes until fragrant.
2. *Adding the Spices:*
   - Stir in the chili powder, cumin, smoked paprika, cayenne pepper, salt, and black pepper. Cook the spices with the onion mixture for about 1 minute to release their flavors.
3. *Simmering the Chili:*
   - Add the black beans, diced tomatoes (with their juice), tomato sauce, and broth to the pot.
   - Stir well to combine, then bring the mixture to a simmer.
   - Reduce the heat to low, cover the pot, and let the chili simmer for 30 minutes, stirring occasionally. This allows the flavors to meld together.

4. *Adjusting the Consistency:*
   - If the chili is too thick, add a little more broth or water to reach your desired consistency.
   - If you prefer a thicker chili, use a potato masher to mash some of the beans directly in the pot.
5. *Serving:*
   - Once the chili is done, taste and adjust the seasoning if necessary.
   - Serve the Spicy Black Bean Chili hot, garnished with fresh cilantro, sour cream, shredded cheese, and lime wedges if desired.

Nutritional Information (per serving): Calories: 250, Total Fat: 8g, Sodium: 700mg, Total Carbohydrates: 37g, Sugars: 5g, Protein: 10g

Tips

- This chili is versatile; you can add vegetables like bell peppers, corn, or zucchini to the mix.
- The chili is even better the next day, as the flavors have more time to develop.
- Serve with cornbread or over rice for a heartier meal.

69: ZHUG-COVERED FALAFEL

Yield: 4 servings	Prep Time: 20 minutes (plus soaking time for chickpeas)	Cook Time: 20 minutes

Ingredients

For the Falafel:

- 1 cup dried chickpeas, soaked overnight
- 1 small onion, chopped
- 3 cloves garlic, minced
- 1/4 cup fresh parsley, chopped
- 1/4 cup fresh cilantro, chopped
- 1 teaspoon ground cumin
- 1 teaspoon ground coriander
- 1/2 teaspoon baking powder
- 1/2 teaspoon salt
- 1/4 teaspoon black pepper
- 2-3 tablespoons flour (if needed)
- Vegetable oil for frying

For the Toppings:

- 1/4 cup Zhug (see recipe 56)
- 1 tablespoon tahini (optional, for drizzling)
- 1/4 cup fresh parsley, chopped (for garnish)
- Pita bread, hummus, and fresh vegetables (for serving)

Instructions

1. *Soaking the Chickpeas:*
   - Place the dried chickpeas in a large bowl and cover with cold water. Allow them to soak overnight (8-12 hours). Drain and rinse the chickpeas before using.
2. *Preparing the Falafel Mixture:*
   - In a food processor, mix the soaked chickpeas, chopped onion, garlic, parsley, cilantro, coriander, cumin, baking powder, salt, and black pepper.
   - Pulse until the mixture is finely ground but not pureed. It should hold together when pressed but still have some texture. If the mixture is too wet, add a little flour to help bind it.
3. *Shaping the Falafel:*
   - Using your hands or a falafel scoop, form the mixture into small balls or patties, about 1 to 1.5 inches in diameter.

4. *Frying the Falafel:*
   - Heat about 2 inches of vegetable oil in a deep skillet or pot over medium heat.
   - Fry the falafel in batches, being careful not to overcrowd the pan. Cook for about 3-4 minutes per side, or until golden brown and crispy. Remove the falafel with a slotted spoon and drain on paper towels.
5. *Drizzling with Zhug:*
   - Arrange the hot falafel balls on a serving platter.
   - Drizzle the Zhug generously over the falafel, making sure each piece is well coated. The Zhug adds a spicy, herby kick to the falafel.
6. *Optional Garnish:*
   - For added flavor, drizzle with tahini and garnish with chopped fresh parsley.
7. *Serving:*
   - Serve the Zhug-covered falafel with warm pita bread, hummus, and fresh vegetables like cucumber, tomatoes, and lettuce.

Nutritional Information (per serving): Calories: 320, Total Fat: 18g, Sodium: 500mg, Total Carbohydrates: 30g, Sugars: 3g, Protein: 10g

Tips

- Ensure that the chickpeas are well soaked to achieve the right texture for the falafel. Do not use canned chickpeas, as they are too soft and will result in mushy falafel.
- If you prefer a baked version, you can brush the falafel with olive oil and bake them in a preheated 375°F (190°C) oven for about 20-25 minutes, turning halfway through.

70: GOCHUJANG GLAZED SALMON

Yield: 4 servings **Prep Time: 10 minutes**
Cook Time:
15-20 minutes

Ingredients

- 4 salmon fillets (6 oz each)
- 3 tablespoons Gochujang (see recipe 54)
- 2 tablespoons soy sauce
- 1 tablespoon honey
- 1 tablespoon sesame oil
- 2 teaspoons rice vinegar
- 2 cloves garlic, minced
- 1 teaspoon grated ginger
- Sesame seeds and chopped green onions (optional, for garnish)

Instructions

1. *Preheating the Oven:*
   - Preheat your oven to 400°F (200°C). Line a baking sheet with parchment paper or lightly grease it with cooking spray.
2. *Making the Glaze:*
   - In a small bowl, stir together the Gochujang, honey, sesame oil, soy sauce, rice vinegar, minced garlic, and grated ginger until well combined.
3. *Preparing the Salmon:*
   - Place the salmon fillets on the prepared baking sheet, skin-side down.
   - Brush the Gochujang glaze generously over each fillet, making sure to coat them evenly.
4. *Baking:*
   - Bake the salmon in the preheated oven for 15-20 minutes, or until the salmon is cooked through and the glaze is caramelized. The salmon should flake easily with a fork.
5. *Serving:*
   - Remove the salmon from the oven and transfer to a serving platter.
   - Serve hot with steamed rice, roasted vegetables, or a fresh salad.

Nutritional Information (per serving): Calories: 300, Total Fat: 15g, Sodium: 800mg, Total Carbohydrates: 10g, Sugars: 6g, Protein: 28g

Tips

- Adjust the sweetness or spice level by adding more or less honey or Gochujang to suit your taste. This glaze also works well with chicken or tofu.

CONCLUSION

As you reach the end of this hot sauce journey, you've not only explored a world of flavors but also gained the tools to create your own spicy masterpieces. Each recipe is a stepping stone, guiding you to experiment, adjust, and perfect your personal heat preferences. Whether you're crafting a sauce to add a subtle kick or one that brings intense fire, the knowledge and techniques shared here will empower you to make each sauce uniquely yours.

Your kitchen is now a playground for bold and exciting flavors. Embrace the creativity that comes with making hot sauce—mixing different peppers, experimenting with spices, and discovering the perfect balance of heat and flavor. Remember, the best hot sauce is the one that satisfies your taste buds and enhances your culinary creations.

As you continue to explore and experiment, your confidence in the kitchen will grow. The recipes you create can bring joy to every meal, sparking conversations and leaving a lasting impression on everyone who tastes your homemade sauces.

May your hot sauce adventures be filled with endless discovery, creativity, and, of course, plenty of heat.

Keep experimenting, and most importantly, enjoy the process!

BONUS!

Dear Reader,
Thank you for exploring the fiery flavors within this book. I hope the recipes and techniques you've discovered will spice up your culinary creations and bring joy to your meals.

As a token of my appreciation for your passion for hot sauce, I am excited to share with you three exclusive bonuses designed to enhance your sauce-making journey and give you a flavorful advantage in your kitchen endeavors.

May your dishes delight and impress, as you bring heat and flavor to the tables of friends and family.
Wishing you a deliciously spicy culinary adventure.

All the best,
Kent Harlen

1. SHOPPING LIST

2. GUIDE TO GROWING AND HARVESTING YOUR OWN CHILI PEPPERS

3. HOW TO START YOUR HOT SAUCE BUSINESS

Get Your Bonuses Here:

**LOOKING FOR MORE RECIPES TO ENJOY YEAR-ROUND?
CHECK OUT THE OTHER 295 RECIPES TO COMPLETE YOUR
COLLECTION OF 365!**

HAPPY COOKING!

https://drive.google.com/file/d/1Cve5ZYKa23smglM0X_8Ce6jN0P94-7Wg/view?usp=sharing

Made in United States
Troutdale, OR
04/08/2025

30456543R00058